One Pot Wonders

1 Pot. 5 Ingredients.
Delicious every time.

One Pot Wonders

GRACE MORTIMER

Contents

Introduction

As someone who now cooks for a living, I often feel trapped in a never-ending loop of cleaning my kitchen. Which is unfortunate because I HATE cleaning. I don't mind a spot of dusting or polishing a mirror, but cleaning my kitchen is something I'm resigned to do five times a day, even when we've not been at home and no one has used the kitchen (no, seriously, where does the mess even come from?) and I can't stand it. It's the only part of cooking I don't enjoy, but eating proper meals is a priority for me, so it has to be done.

Whenever I speak to people about cooking (something I'm told I do a lot), and they tell me they don't enjoy it, the most common reason is usually something along the lines of 'it's a faff'. When you dig a little deeper, that 'faff' often refers to hunting down a long list of ingredients, measuring everything out, tackling all the chopping, peeling and prepping – and, of course, the dreaded washing up afterwards.

Here's the good news: this book is designed to take the faff out of cooking. With just five ingredients or fewer per recipe – many of them already portioned (think tins, packets or whole items like onions or peppers) – there's far less to worry about. And as for the washing up? No, I'm not offering to come and do it for you, but I have supplied you with recipes that use only ONE pot, ONE pan, ONE tray or other vessel. And we're not cheating here; this isn't a case of using a frying pan first, then transferring everything to a slow cooker, or boiling pasta and then adding it to the sauce you've made in another saucepan – this really is all in one.

Why five ingredients?

Those of you who follow me on social media or own copies of my previous books will know that all my recipes contain five ingredients or fewer. Why? Well, put simply, it's this: being an adult means life is already full of long and complicated lists of things to do, so let's not add to it. I'm not a miracle worker, but my aim is to make mealtimes just that bit more manageable.

I create recipes using run-of-the-mill ingredients you probably already have, without the use of fancy equipment and with minimal effort, process or time required. I don't count things like sunflower oil or salt and pepper as part of the five ingredients – I consider them staples that we all have in our kitchens. Instead, you'll find them listed separately under a 'for cooking' section in each recipe.

This book is my easiest yet. Most recipes generally go like this: ***'Add these five things to a tray, put the tray in the oven for half an hour, remove the tray, eat the food.'*** The goal, if you like, is to create delicious meals that are so simple and memorably tasty, you only need to follow the recipe the first time you try them. After that, you've probably got it committed to memory. And perhaps next time you can put your own twist on it. Got some spare veg lying around looking forlorn in the bottom of your fridge? Add it to the curry. Run out of cumin? Don't fret, whatever dried spice you like and have in stock – use that instead! That's how mealtimes in my house go 95% of the time.

Why one pot?

In my ongoing mission to make mealtimes easier, this book felt like the natural next step. In terms of ingredients, we can't get any simpler than sticking to the five. In terms of process, I've always limited this to as little as feasibly possible. But my recipes have got even easier again, because using only one vessel to cook an entire meal means that, once you've got your five ingredients laid out in front of you, plus the pan or tray you're using, you're ready to go. This not only saves time and washing up, it's just less to think about.

I think one of the reasons that ready meals appear so attractive to us when we're exhausted, busy and time is of the essence, is because it means no washing up afterwards. You simply heat them, eat them and throw the packaging away. I'm not judging anyone whatsoever for opting for the occasional ready meal (we all do it, myself included). But at a time when we're all being encouraged to reduce our waste and keep a tight hold on the purse strings, if I can provide you with recipes that save you time, money and washing up, not to mention them being a heck of a lot more delicious, then I'll have achieved what I set out to do here.

Just because something is simple does not make it inferior. Cooking can be as simple or as complicated as you make it! A lot of the time I see a great recipe I'd love to attempt, but buying all the ingredients and following three pages of steps will stop me in my tracks. Some of the best food I've ever eaten has been in Italy, where a few simple ingredients are elevated with the use of good-quality olive oil and a pinch of salt. A bowl of spaghetti tastes like heaven because good vine-ripened tomatoes have been used, plus more garlic than seems humanly possible to consume, with both coming together to make a rich, flavoursome sauce. This is simple done well, in my opinion. Good ingredients and good seasoning go a long way, and while you can opt for molecular gastronomy if that happens to be your inclination, I don't think many of us have the time or means for it. This book is simple. Simple done well.

Love, Grace x

Symbols

Vegetarian

These vegetarian recipes are all about fresh, wholesome ingredients. I promise you won't miss the meat.

Frying Pan

Quick, easy and flavoursome, these recipes are crowd-pleasing meals you'll have on the table in no time at all, using only the humble frying pan. The bigger the pan, the better!

Traybake

Everyone loves a traybake! Find me someone who doesn't like them and I'll change their mind – guaranteed.

One Bowl

This is as easy as it gets. You are literally chopping things up and chucking them in a bowl. Think big, colourful one-bowl recipes, which come together in a matter of minutes.

Saucepan

These recipes are for when you haven't really got time to stand at the stove and tend to the food, but you want something quick and wholesome.

Air Fryer

Cheap, speedy, healthy and so versatile – I must say I LOVE my air fryer. These are delicious recipes you'll be amazed you can make in it without the use of any other equipment.

Roasting Pot

Now, when I talk about roasting pots, I mean lidded dishes that go in the oven. However, if you don't have a dish like this, then you can use a deep oven tray and cover it tightly with foil, then follow these recipes exactly as they're written.

Slow Cooker

The ultimate dump-and-run meals! What could be nicer than walking through your front door after a long day at work and thinking, 'Not only will dinner be ready in one minute, but it's hot and it smells amazing.'

Morphy
Richards
HIGH
LOW
OFF
MED
CAUTION HOT SURFACE

Shopping List

Keeping your freezer and pantry stocked with the right ingredients makes cooking a breeze. By having a few key items on hand, you'll save time on grocery trips and ensure you're always ready to whip up something tasty.

Here are some of my favourite freezer and store-cupboard ingredients I recommend keeping in stock or adding to your shopping list:

Canned goods

- Tinned tomatoes
- Tinned chickpeas/beans
- Coconut milk

Seasoning

- Curry powder
- Stock cubes

Frozen food

- Frozen veg (peas, sweetcorn, spinach, mixed veg)
- Frozen prawns

Sauces

- Pesto
- Thai curry paste
- Harissa paste
- Soy sauce

Dried foods

- Dried pasta
- Dried gnocchi
- Dried noodles
- Basmati rice

Weekly Meal Planner

	Monday	Tuesday	Wednesday
Breakfast	Breakfast Hash (page 30)	Breakfast Muffins (page 22)	Breakfast Pie (page 28)
Lunch	Smoky Carrot Soup (page 51)	Tomatoey Tuna Salad with Pesto Dressing (page 60)	Mexican Stuffed Falafel (page 192)
Dinner	Mediterranean Cod & Lentils with Olive Salsa (page 88)	Cheesy Cajun Chicken (page 80)	Honey Mustard Roast Salmon with Chips (page 90)
Dessert	Fruit and yoghurt	Fruit & Nut Energy Bars (page 221)	Bakewell Tart Fudge (page 210)

Here is an example meal plan. Don't worry – you don't have to cook more than 20 different meals each week! But if you're someone who likes to plan your meals, this is a useful template to follow. I've also given you a blank template on page 228, so that you can plan your own menus once you've figured out what works for your family. Photocopy it and stick it to your fridge for easy reference.

Thursday	Friday	Saturday	Sunday
Smoky Butter Bean Shakshuka (page 20)	Chocolate & Banana Baked Oats (page 29)	Harissa Fried Egg with Avocado Flatbread (page 26)	Brie & Cranberry Pancakes (page 25)
Whipped Feta & Avocado Salad (page 72)	Halloumi Salad with Crispy Chickpeas (page 52)	Crunchy Asian Noodle Salad (page 34)	Italian Lemon Chicken (page 130)
Chicken & Cauliflower Peanut Butter Curry (page 164)	Bolognese Loaded Flatbreads (page 44)	Crispy Sage & Chestnut Gnocchi (page 46)	Slow-Cooked Lamb & Beans (page 162)
leftover Bakewell Tart Fudge (page 210)	Lemon Posset (page 218)	Salted Caramel Ice Cream (page 214)	Fruit & Nut Energy Bars (page 221)

Breakfast

Smoky Butter Bean Shakshuka

Frying Pan

Vegetarian

Serves 2–3

This is one of those meals I make with every intention of sharing but somehow end up eating half of (directly from the pan, burning my mouth multiple times) before I've served it... Harissa and feta are very good friends and should hang out more often, trust me! And for this meal, toast makes an excellent companion.

- 1 x 400g (14oz) tin of butter beans
- 1 x 400g (14oz) tin of chopped tomatoes
- 2 tbsp harissa paste
- 2 or 3 eggs
- 1 handful of crumbled feta

FOR COOKING
sunflower oil

1 Add the butter beans (including the liquid from the tin), tomatoes and harissa, along with a little oil, to a wide-based frying pan over a low heat and bring everything to a gentle simmer.

2 Using a spoon, make 2 or 3 wells in the mixture and crack the eggs into the wells. Pop the lid on and leave over a low heat for 5 minutes, until the egg whites are opaque and set – leave it a little longer if you like your yolks firm.

3 Remove the lid, sprinkle the feta over the top and serve.

Breakfast Muffins

Traybake

Makes 6

Whenever I go to a coffee shop and see the price of their savoury breakfast muffins, I nearly abandon my hot drink and march out in protest! They are so expensive and often under-seasoned and lacking in texture and taste – and are usually far too small to be considered 'breakfast' in my opinion. If you share my sentiments, then I highly encourage you to make your own. These are delicious, filling and make a great grab-and-dash breakfast for anyone having a hectic morning.

- 100g (3½oz) diced ham
- 1 handful of small cheddar cubes
- 1 handful of chopped chives, plus extra to garnish
- 3 sundried tomatoes, finely diced
- 3 eggs

FOR GREASING
- butter

1. Preheat the oven to 200°C (180°C fan).
2. Add all the ingredients to a large bowl and mix thoroughly.
3. Grease a 6-cup muffin tray, and divide the mixture evenly into the moulds.
4. Bake for 20 minutes. Remove and leave to cool for 20 minutes before removing from the moulds. Garnish with extra chives.

Brie & Cranberry Pancakes

Frying Pan

Vegetarian

Makes 10–12

Why not combine the makings of my favourite sandwich and turn it into pancakes! A fantastic cure for cold winter mornings and the perfect way to use up any leftover brie you might have lurking in the cheese drawer (she says, as if there is such a thing as leftover brie..!)

- 1 egg
- 1 cup (125g/4½oz) self-raising flour
- 1 cup (250ml/8fl oz) milk, any
- 100g (3½oz) brie, diced into small cubes
- 3 heaped tbsp cranberry sauce

FOR COOKING
- sunflower oil

1. Combine all the ingredients in a large bowl and mix thoroughly.
2. Add a drizzle of oil to a hot frying pan. Scoop in ladle-sized amounts of the mixture.
3. Fry until golden on both sides. Serve with generous dollops of cranberry sauce.

Harissa Fried Egg with Avocado Flatbread

Frying Pan

Vegetarian

Serves 2

This is the sort of breakfast you'd order at a fancy brunch but feel a bit miffed because they didn't add enough avocado or perhaps you wanted more harissa or maybe the egg wasn't cooked to your liking. Well, don't waste your money and make it at home just the way you like it! Plus, you get to drink your tea or coffee out of your favourite mug. We've all got one.

- 150g (5oz) plain yoghurt (plus 1 extra tbsp)
- 150g (5oz) self-raising flour
- 1 avocado
- 1 tbsp harissa paste
- 2 eggs

FOR COOKING
sunflower oil

1. In a large bowl, combine the yoghurt and flour and bring together to form a pliable dough. If it's too crumbly, add a little extra yoghurt to bind it. If too wet, add a little extra flour. Split the dough into 2 even balls. On a floured surface, use a rolling pin to roll the dough out into rough circles approximately as thick as a pound coin.
2. Add the breads to a hot frying pan with a tiny drizzle of oil and fry on both sides until golden (you'll know when they're ready to flip because the breads will puff up).
3. Meanwhile, peel, destone and mash the avocado in a bowl, then combine it with 1 tbsp of yoghurt to form a thick avocado dip. Season if you wish.
4. Once the flatbreads are cooked, remove and set aside for a moment. To the same hot frying pan add the harissa along with a good drizzle of oil. Immediately crack the eggs on top of the hot harissa oil.
5. Once the eggs are cooked, divide the avocado dip between the two breads and spread evenly, then place an egg on top of each one. Drizzle with extra harissa oil and season with salt and pepper to taste.

Breakfast Pie

Serves 4

Breakfast, lunch or dinner – everyone will enjoy this! It's seriously hearty fare and couldn't be easier to make.

- 6–8 sausages
- 1 x 400g (14oz) tin of baked beans
- 1 x 400g (14oz) tin of chopped tomatoes
- 2 handfuls of grated Cheddar
- 12 frozen hash browns

FOR COOKING
sunflower oil

1 Preheat the oven to 200°C (180°C fan).

2 Add the sausages to an ovenproof dish with a little oil and bake in the hot oven for 15 minutes.

3 Remove from the oven, tip the beans and tomatoes over the sausages and give everything a good mix. Sprinkle over half the grated cheese, then arrange the frozen hash browns across the top.

4 Finally, top with the remaining grated cheese and place back in the oven for a further 25 minutes, then serve.

Chocolate & Banana Baked Oats

Traybake

Vegetarian

Serves 4–6

These are more like breakfast brownies than baked oats. Super-squishy and moist with pockets of gooey melted chocolate and crispy flapjack-like edges.

- 2 cups (90g/3¼oz) oat flour
- 3 eggs
- 3 ripe bananas, mashed
- 100g (3½oz) chocolate chips
- 100ml (3½fl oz) maple syrup

1. Preheat the oven to 200°C (180°C fan).
2. Combine all the ingredients and mix thoroughly.
3. Line an ovenproof tray (about 20cm x 20cm x 5cm) with baking paper. Pour in the mixture and smooth out.
4. Bake for 20 minutes. Remove from the oven and leave to cool for 10 minutes before slicing. Enjoy!

To make the oat flour, add 2 cups (180g/6½oz) regular porridge oats to a food processor and blitz until it looks like flour.

Breakfast Hash

Frying Pan

Serves 4

Controversial statement incoming... I'm actually not a fan of the classic British fry-up. Don't get me wrong, I can see its merit when you've perhaps had a late night and, come the morning, you're feeling a little 'tired and emotional'. But otherwise it gives me indigestion for most of the day and I feel sluggish and sleepy by lunchtime. This recipe takes elements from the fry-up: egg, sausage, beans, tomatoes, fried potatoes, but somehow ends up feeling healthier, less oily and takes considerably less time to make!

- 2 medium potatoes, cut into small (1cm/½ inch) cubes (unpeeled)
- 6–8 sausages, cut into chunks
- 1 x 400g (14oz) tin of chopped tomatoes
- 1 x 400g (14oz) tin of cannellini beans, rinsed and drained
- 4 eggs

FOR COOKING

- sunflower oil

1. Add the potatoes to a large frying pan with a little oil over a medium heat, and fry until golden and crispy on the outside.
2. Add the sausages to the potatoes and move them around in the pan regularly, until the sausages have browned and the potatoes crisp up on all sides.
3. Turn the heat down to low and add the tomatoes and beans. Give everything a good stir and bring the whole lot to a simmer. At this point check the seasoning and add salt and pepper if you wish.
4. Once simmering, make 4 wells using a spoon, and crack the eggs into the wells.
5. Cover the pan (with foil if you don't have a lid) and let it bubble away for about 5 minutes, until the egg whites are opaque and set – leave it a little longer if you like your yolks firm. Serve and enjoy!

Easy

Lunches

Crunchy Asian Noodle Salad

Serves 2

No soggy salads, please! This is a great one to make ahead of the week and store in jars or Tupperware for quick, delicious lunches. It is fantastic on its own, or lovely with sticky ribs, slow-cooked meat or a BBQ.

- 2 carrots, peeled
- 60g (2¼oz) red cabbage, shredded
- 50g (1¾oz) dried vermicelli rice noodles
- 3 tbsp peanut butter (I used smooth but crunchy works too!)
- 1 tbsp soy sauce

1 Chop the carrots into thin batons (alternatively, use a julienne peeler or a conventional swivel peeler to slice them lengthways into strips or ribbons), then add them to a large bowl along with the red cabbage.

2 Place the noodles in a large heatproof bowl, pour over enough boiling water to cover and leave to stand for 5 minutes.

3 Meanwhile, combine the peanut butter, soy sauce and 1 tablespoon of boiling water in a jug. Whisk until you have a thick dressing.

4 Once the noodles have softened, drain and add them to the carrot and cabbage. Pour over the dressing and give it a good mix. Enjoy!

Beetroot & Blood Orange Salad

Serves 2

This salad looks rather fancy but is incredibly quick and simple to assemble. It's exactly the sort of salad you should serve in that pretty dish you don't normally use (for fear of it getting chipped or dropped) and offer up to guests who will say things like, 'Gosh, look at this salad, you've gone to such a lot of effort,' and you will reply, 'Oh, it's no trouble really,' and feel rather smug and brilliant.

- 2 cooked beetroot, diced
- 2 blood oranges (or regular oranges if not in season)
- 100g (3½oz) goat's cheese
- 1 handful of chopped almonds
- few sprigs of mint, leaves only

FOR COOKING AND TO FINISH
olive oil

1. Add the diced beetroot to a large bowl.
2. Using a knife, pare one of the oranges and slice into rounds, then add the rounds to the beetroot.
3. Slice the goat's cheese into generous rounds. Combine with the beetroot and orange, then sprinkle the chopped almonds across the top.
4. Slice the remaining orange in half then squeeze the juice into a jug. Add a tablespoon of olive oil, season with a little salt and pepper and whisk together.
5. Drizzle the dressing across the top of the salad and top with the mint leaves.

Fried Halloumi & Spiced Plum Salad

Serves 2

Fried halloumi is the gift that keeps on giving, and I'm genuinely suspicious of people who say they don't like it… aren't you? And it pairs so well with sticky, spicy plums!

- 3 or 4 plums, halved and destoned
- 1 tbsp ground cumin
- 100g (3½oz) halloumi, cut into cubes
- ½ cup (55g/2oz) plain yoghurt
- 1 handful of chopped parsley

FOR COOKING AND TO FINISH
olive oil

1 In a large bowl, combine the plums, cumin and good glug of olive oil. Mix until coated on all sides.

2 Add the halloumi to a hot frying pan with a drizzle of oil and fry until golden and crispy on all sides. Remove from the pan.

3 Next, turn the heat down to medium and add the plums, skin side up, to the frying pan. Fry for a few minutes before flipping them over. Add a splash of cold water if they are starting to smoke and turn the heat off once the skins are starting to break down but they are still maintaining their shape.

4 Spread the yoghurt out on a large plate to act as a base for the salad. Spoon over the cooked plums and add a little of the cooking juices.

5 Sprinkle the halloumi and parsley across the top and drizzle over a little olive oil at the end. Season if you wish and serve!

Huevos Rancheros

Frying Pan

Vegetarian

Serves 4

This is something I've only recently discovered and, oh my goodness, where have I actually been?! Such a cheap, delicious and speedy lunch.

- 4 tortilla wraps
- 1 x 400g (14oz) tin of black beans, drained
- 2 tbsp chipotle paste
- 4 eggs
- 1 avocado, peeled, destoned and finely sliced

FOR COOKING

- sunflower oil

1 One at a time, add the tortillas to a hot, dry frying pan and cook on both sides until slightly coloured and crispy in places, then set aside.

2 Add a little oil to the pan, then add the beans. Cook all the water out of them, then mash and add a little water. Continue mashing and adding a little water until you get a coarse, refried bean texture. Spoon the bean mixture onto the tortillas.

3 Wipe the pan clean then add a little oil, plus 1 teaspoon of chipotle paste per egg and mix together. Fry the eggs on top of the chipotle oil mixture.

4 Finally, place the eggs on top of the beans and add a few slices of avocado.

5 Drizzle a little of the remaining chipotle paste on top of each one, garnish with pepper and serve.

Roasted Peppers Stuffed with Cheesy Lentils

Serves 4

Filling, delicious and easy to make. This is a very budget-friendly meal with lovely, garlicky, cheesy lentils that taste even better roasted inside a sweet pepper.

- 1 x 400g (14oz) tin of lentils, drained
- 1 cup (140g/4¾oz) sweetcorn
- 4 spring onions, finely sliced
- 100g (3½oz) garlic roule/Boursin cheese
- 4 peppers (red, yellow or orange)

1. Preheat the oven to 200°C (180°C fan).
2. In a large bowl, combine the lentils, sweetcorn, spring onions and garlic cheese. Mix thoroughly and check for seasoning.
3. Slice the tops off the peppers and remove the seeds. Spoon the lentil mixture into each pepper until full, then place the pepper lids back on top.
4. Place the peppers upright in a roasting pot so they're packed together.
5. Pop the lid on the pot and bake in the oven for 45 minutes, then remove the lid and return to the oven for 15 minutes, before serving.

If the pot is too big, take a sheet of foil and roll it into one long sausage, then cut it into 4 and turn the scrunched foil strips into O shapes, so the peppers can sit on top of them to stop them from falling over.

Potato, Cheese & Onion Pasties

Serves 4

Comfort food 101. I've been trying to make the perfect potato, cheese and onion pasty since I tried them in that famous bakery we all frequent. While these three things combined are delicious as they are, the dash of Worcestershire sauce really makes them sing!

- 1 x 565g (1lb 4oz) tin of potatoes, drained
- 1 red onion, finely diced
- 1 cup (115g/4oz) grated Cheddar
- 1 tbsp Worcestershire sauce
- 1 x 320g (11¼oz) sheet of puff pastry

FOR BRUSHING

- 1 beaten egg or a little milk

1. Add the potatoes to a large bowl and use a fork or potato masher to break them down into smaller chunks. Add the red onion, Cheddar and Worcestershire sauce and mix thoroughly.

2. Lay the sheet of puff pastry on a flat surface and cut it lengthways into 4 rectangles.

3. Add the filling to one end of each rectangle and fold over the other end, then use a fork to crimp down the sides to stop any filling from falling out.

4. Transfer the pasties to your air fryer and use a pastry brush to brush with beaten egg or milk. Cook at 200°C for 20 minutes, until golden brown, then remove and enjoy!

Bolognese Loaded Flatbreads

Serves 4

Do you ever find yourself repeatedly buying mince and then thinking, now what? If you're anything like me, it usually turns into a Bolognese or a cottage pie, but this is a great way to either use up leftover Bolognese sauce or simply change things up a bit with lovely, fluffy homemade wraps. The wraps can even be packaged in foil and taken on a picnic!

- 2 cups (220g/7¾oz) plain yoghurt
- 2 cups (260g/9¼oz) self-raising flour, plus extra for dusting
- 500g (1lb 2oz) beef mince
- 500g (1lb 2oz) passata
- 1 handful of grated Cheddar

FOR COOKING
sunflower oil

1. In a large bowl, combine the yoghurt and flour and bring the mixture together to form a pliable dough. If it's too wet, add a little extra flour; too dry and crumbly, add a little extra yoghurt.
2. On a floured surface, use a rolling pin to roll the dough into 4–6 flatbreads, then add them one at a time to a frying pan with a little oil over a medium heat. Once the bread starts to bubble and puff up, it's ready to flip. Cook on both sides until cooked all the way through, then set them aside.
3. Rinse the pan out then brown off the mince with a little oil and cook until the liquid has evaporated. Add the passata and reduce the heat to a simmer. Stirring occasionally, bring everything to a gentle simmer and cook for 15 minutes, until the mixture is almost starting to dry out. Check for seasoning.
4. Finally, assemble the dish by spooning some Bolognese onto each flatbread, followed by a little grated cheese, and enjoy!

Crispy Sage & Chestnut Gnocchi

Frying Pan

Vegetarian

Serves 4

I had this in Italy when I was pregnant with my son, Harry, and it was so memorable I've been making it ever since! Unless a dish contains meat, my partner, Tom, thinks it's basically a side salad. Sometimes I add a little chorizo or sausage to make it Tom-friendly, but Harry and I often have this for lunch during the school holidays, because we both love it.

- 5–6 sage leaves
- 500g (1lb 2oz) gnocchi
- 180g (6½oz) cooked chestnuts, roughly chopped
- 1 cup (130g/4½oz) defrosted peas
- 1 handful of grated Parmesan

FOR COOKING
- olive oil

1. Add a good drizzle of oil to a hot frying pan, add the sage leaves and fry until firm and crispy; remove from the pan.
2. Add the gnocchi to the pan and fry until golden and crispy on all sides, then add the chestnuts, peas and a little glug of water. Reduce the heat to a simmer and stir regularly to ensure everything is piping hot.
3. Finally, crumble in the sage leaves and add the grated Parmesan, along with a drizzle of olive oil, and give it one final toss together.
4. Once the Parmesan has melted, plate up, pop any leftover sage leaves on top and you're ready to eat!

Hot Sweet Potato Salad

Serves 4

Sweet roasted cherry tomatoes, crispy chickpeas, caramelised sweet potato and tangy melted feta – this is a lovely combination. Perfect as a side dish or the main event, and a good way to use up leftovers in the fridge to create something delicious and full of goodness.

- 2 large sweet potatoes, cut into about 2cm (¾ inch) cubes (unpeeled)
- 1 x 400g (14oz) tin of chickpeas, drained
- 2 handfuls of cherry tomatoes
- 1 tbsp smoked paprika
- 1 handful of crumbled feta

FOR COOKING
sunflower oil

1 Preheat the oven to 200°C (180°C fan).

2 Add the sweet potatoes, chickpeas, cherry tomatoes and smoked paprika to a large ovenproof dish, with a drizzle of oil, and give it a good mix so the paprika has coated everything.

3 Bake in the oven for 40 minutes, then sprinkle the feta across the top and bake for a further 10 minutes, or until the cheese is starting to melt and turn slightly golden.

4 Remove from the oven, give it one final mix, season if you wish and serve!

Smoky Carrot Soup

Serves 4

Carrots make such great soup – they're naturally sweet, blend into a silky-smooth texture, and they go with just about any spices you can think of. This is simple, delicious and extremely cheap to make!

- 400g (14oz) carrots, peeled and roughly chopped
- 2 tbsp harissa paste
- 2 red onions, sliced
- 1 vegetable stock cube
- good drizzle of single cream

1. Add the carrots to the slow cooker along with the harissa, onions, stock cube and 250ml (1 cup/8fl oz) boiling water.
2. Cook on high for 6 hours, then add another 200ml (7fl oz) boiling water and use a stick blender to blitz until smooth.
3. Spoon into bowls and drizzle some cream over the top to serve.

To adapt this for the stove, roast the carrots first for extra flavour, then sauté the onions and spices in a pot, add the carrots and stock, and simmer until tender. Blend and hey presto.

Halloumi Salad with Crispy Chickpeas

Air Fryer

Vegetarian

Serves 4

Halloumi and tahini is such a fantastic combination; there's a reason you see them together in recipes all over the internet!

- 1 x 400g (14oz) tin of chickpeas, rinsed, drained and patted dry
- 150g (5oz) halloumi, cut into chunks or strips
- 3 tbsp tahini
- 1 baby gem lettuce, finely sliced
- 1 red onion, finely sliced

FOR COOKING
sunflower oil

1. Add the chickpeas with a drizzle of oil to your air fryer and cook at 200°C for 10 minutes until crispy. Remove and set aside.
2. Meanwhile, add the halloumi to a bowl, drizzle over most of the tahini plus a drizzle of oil and toss until coated.
3. Add the halloumi pieces to your air fryer for 10 minutes until golden, giving them a toss halfway through so they cook evenly.
4. To assemble the salad, arrange the lettuce in a large bowl or plate, followed by the onion, then top with the halloumi and crispy chickpeas. Finally, drizzle the remaining tahini across the top and season if you wish.

If you would rather have cooked onions in your salad as opposed to raw, add them to the air fryer along with the halloumi, tahini and oil.

Feta 'Scramble' with Crispy Salmon

Serves 4

Feta 'scramble' is my go-to working-from-home lunch. I really like it with salmon, but sometimes I'll have it with leftover roast chicken or perhaps a fried egg. It's quick, healthy and delicious!

- 4 skin-on salmon fillets
- 2 handfuls of cherry tomatoes, halved
- 500g (1lb 2oz) spinach leaves
- 200g (7oz) feta, crumbled
- 4 slices of toast

FOR COOKING
- oil spray

1. Use kitchen towel to pat dry the salmon. Drizzle a little oil in the base of the air fryer, then add the salmon, skin-side down, along with the tomatoes. Cook at 200°C for 10 minutes, until the salmon is cooked to your liking. Remove the salmon from the air fryer.

2. Add the spinach and feta to the tomatoes, give them a really good mix and air fry for a further 2 minutes.

3. Give it one final stir then spoon the feta scramble onto the slices of toast and top with the crispy-skin salmon.

Salmon & Crispy Potatoes with Mustard Mayo

Air Fryer

Serves 4

This combination is perfection! Need I say more?

- 2 x 565g (1lb 4oz) tins of potatoes, drained
- 4 skin-on salmon fillets
- 2 tbsp wholegrain mustard
- 5 tbsp mayonnaise
- 1 red onion, sliced

FOR COOKING
oil spray

1. Add the potatoes to your air fryer along with a spritz of oil and cook at 200°C for 10 minutes.
2. Add the salmon fillets skin-side down, and cook for a further 10 minutes, until the salmon is cooked to your liking and the potatoes are golden and crispy.
3. Meanwhile, combine the mustard and mayonnaise in a bowl and mix thoroughly.
4. Once the potatoes and salmon are done, put the potatoes in a large bowl and place the salmon fillets on top. Use a fork to flake the salmon into chunks.
5. Scatter over the onion and top with the mayonnaise dressing. Give everything a good mix and you're ready to eat!

Cheesy Kimchi Fried Rice

Serves 2

Kimchi is one of those ingredients that can take a little getting used to, but it's so good for you, and once you start eating it you won't be able to stop! This is a great way of introducing the flavour to the rest of your family in a very accessible way, and the combination of kimchi and melted tangy cheese is simply the best.

- 1 egg
- 1 cup (150g/5oz) frozen mixed veg
- 1 x 250g (9oz) packet of microwave rice
- 150g (5oz) kimchi, plus 1 tbsp liquid from the jar
- 1 handful of grated cheese (any type)

FOR COOKING
sunflower oil

1. Crack the egg into a hot frying pan with a little oil. Fry until cooked through, using a wooden spoon or spatula to break it down into chunks.
2. Stir in the frozen veg, rice and the tablespoon of kimchi liquid.
3. Fry until everything is piping hot and starting to catch, then turn the heat down to low and add the kimchi. Give it a good stir, allowing the liquid from the kimchi to deglaze the pan. Add the grated cheese, stir through and take off the heat.
4. Once the cheese has melted, serve with extra kimchi on the side.

Tomatoey Tuna Salad with Pesto Dressing

One Bowl

Serves 1

This is exactly the sort of thing I make for myself for lunch when I haven't got a lot of time. I often double up the ingredients to make even more portions to store for a quick grab-and-go healthy meal.

- 1 x 145g (5oz) tin of tuna, drained
- 2 handfuls of cherry tomatoes, chopped
- 1 handful of crumbled feta
- ½ red onion, finely sliced
- 2 tbsp sundried tomato pesto

1. Add the tuna, tomatoes, feta and red onion to a large bowl and mix together.
2. Spoon the pesto into a jug and loosen with a little water, season generously and drizzle over the salad. That's all there is to it!

Coconut Lentils with Cauliflower & Spiced Halloumi

Serves 4

Healthy and comforting, I love to make a batch of this and keep it in the fridge for easy grab-and-reheat lunches throughout the week. Ultra-filling and full of goodness!

- 100g (3½oz) halloumi, cut into about 2cm (¾ inch) cubes
- 3 tbsp curry powder
- 1 cauliflower, cut into florets
- 2 x 400g (14oz) tins of lentils, drained
- 1 x 400g (14oz) tin of full-fat coconut milk

FOR COOKING
sunflower oil

1 Add the halloumi to a large bowl with 1 tablespoon of the curry powder and a drizzle of oil and toss until each halloumi cube is coated.

2 Add a drizzle of oil and the halloumi to a large saucepan over a medium heat. Fry until golden on all sides, then remove the halloumi.

3 Stir in the cauliflower to the same pan and sauté until slightly coloured, then add the remaining curry powder, along with the lentils.

4 Turn the heat down to low and simmer until the mixture is starting to dry out, at which point stir through the coconut milk and leave over a low heat for about 10 minutes, until the mixture is thick and creamy. Check for seasoning, adding any if you feel it needs it.

5 Spoon into bowls and top with the warm halloumi cubes.

Butternut Squash & Butter Bean Traybake

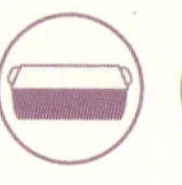

Traybake

Vegetarian

Serves 4

This is what I call an 'end of the veg' meal. You know the ones I mean: when you've got a vegetable drawer full of slightly limp vegetables that have probably seen better days but are still good for eating. Simply chuck them in the oven with a tin of butter beans to crisp up, and drizzle with pesto. Perfect as a healthy meal in its own right, or a delicious accompaniment to a roast.

- 1 butternut squash, deseeded and sliced (skin on or off, it doesn't matter)
- 2 red onions, roughly chopped
- 1 x 400g (14oz) tin of butter beans, drained
- 2 handfuls of chopped kale
- 2 heaped tbsp pesto

FOR COOKING

- sunflower oil

1. Preheat the oven to 220°C (200°C fan).
2. Add the butternut squash, onions and butter beans to a large tray, along with a drizzle of oil, and bake for 30 minutes.
3. Remove the tray from the oven, add the kale and pesto, give everything a good mix, place foil over the top of the tray and return to the oven for 5 minutes.
4. Remove from the oven, season if you wish, and serve!

'With a BBQ' Couscous Jumble

Serves 4

I always I seem to make this with a barbecue and it is, indeed, a jumble! We tend to spatchcock a whole chicken and cook it slowly over coals, then slice the cooked, hot chicken and serve it on top of this salad. Give it a go!

- 1 cup (170g/6oz) dried couscous
- 1 apple, cored and finely diced
- 100g (3½oz) feta, crumbled
- 1 handful of rocket leaves
- 1 tbsp pesto, whisked with 2 tbsp olive oil

TO FINISH
olive oil

1 Place the couscous in a large heatproof bowl and pour over enough boiling water to cover (and not more). Pop a plate or clingfilm over the top to allow it to steam and cook for 2 minutes. Use a fork to fluff it up and season if you wish.

2 Add the couscous to a large bowl and allow to cool for 10 minutes, then add the apple, feta and rocket and give it a good mix together.

3 Whisk the pesto with 2 tbsp olive oil to form a dressing and season with salt and pepper if you wish, then drizzle it over the salad and give it one final mix.

Smashed Parmesan Potatoes with Smoked Mackerel

Air Fryer

Serves 4

Smashed Parmesan potatoes cooked in the air fryer is a dish in its own right, but paired with flaky smoked mackerel, crispy green beans and crunchy red onion, it's a gorgeous combination!

- 1 x 565g (1lb 4oz) tin of potatoes, drained
- 1 handful of green beans, halved
- 2 handfuls of grated Parmesan
- 1 red onion, sliced
- 2 smoked mackerel fillets, flaked into chunks

FOR COOKING AND TO FINISH
olive oil

1. Add the potatoes to the air fryer with a good drizzle of olive oil and cook at 200°C for 15 minutes, until starting to crisp up on the outside.
2. Use the bottom of a glass or mug to crush each potato. Cover with another drizzle of oil, add the beans and sprinkle half the Parmesan across the top of everything. Air-fry for a further 5 minutes, until the potatoes are crisp.
3. Spoon the potatoes and beans into a large bowl and scatter over the red onion. Place the smoked mackerel chunks on top.
4. In a small bowl, combine the remaining Parmesan with a drizzle of olive oil and drizzle across everything to serve. An extra sprinkle of Parmesan on top adds a nice touch.

Stuffed Crust Chorizo Pizza

Serves 4

What's better than cheesy chorizo pizza? Cheesy chorizo pizza with extra melted cheese stuffed in at the sidelines! This is an all-round crowd pleaser.

- 1 x 320g (11¼oz) sheet of puff pastry
- 2 x 125g (4½oz) balls of mozzarella, torn into chunks
- 2–3 tbsp ready-made pizza base sauce
- 2 red onions, finely sliced
- 1 handful of sliced chorizo

FOR BRUSHING

1 beaten egg or a little milk

1 Preheat the oven to 220°C (200°C fan).

2 Lay the puff pastry sheet on a baking tray lined with baking parchment.

3 Arrange half the mozzarella in a line all around the edge of the pastry. Use your fingers to fold over the pastry edges, enclosing the mozzarella to form the stuffed crust.

4 Spoon the pizza sauce across the middle of the pastry and sprinkle the red onions on top.

5 Scatter the chorizo slices evenly across the pizza and top with the remaining chunks of mozzarella.

6 Use a pastry brush to brush beaten egg or milk over the stuffed crust edge, then cook in the oven for 25 minutes, until golden and crispy on top. Remove, slice and serve!

Whipped Feta & Avocado Salad

Serves 2

I'm a sucker for creamy salad dressings, and anything with whipped feta is basically okay with me. The issue I've had with this salad is trying not to eat all the dressing directly from the blender with a spoon before I've assembled the salad!

- 2 avocados, peeled and destoned
- 2 tbsp plain yoghurt
- 100g (3½oz) feta
- 1 x 400g (14oz) tin of chickpeas, rinsed and drained
- 1 red onion, finely sliced

1. Add one of the avocados to a blender along with the yoghurt and half the feta. Blitz until you have a smooth, creamy dressing, seasoning if you wish.
2. Cut the remaining avocado into chunks.
3. Tip the chickpeas, onion and avocado into a bowl and drizzle over the dressing. Tumble together and serve!

Cretan Dakos Salad

One Bowl

Vegetarian

Serves 4

Is it possible to live off dakos salad for a month and nothing else? Well, actually, yes it is... how do I know this? Because I've accidentally tried it! Many moons ago I travelled through the Greek Islands and spent nearly a month in Crete because it's the biggest of all the islands and there was so much to see. Being on an incredibly tight budget, and because this was the cheapest thing on any menu, I ate it for lunch and dinner for nearly a month in order to be able to afford beer (or retsina, yikes)! It's nostalgic, surprisingly filling and totally delicious. For maximum flavour, use tomatoes that are ripe and juicy.

- 2 slices of brown bread
- 2 handfuls of cherry tomatoes, chopped
- 1 handful of pitted black olives
- 100g (3½oz) feta, crumbled
- good glug of olive oil

1. Toast the bread in the toaster then rip into chunks with your hands.
2. Place the toast pieces in a large bowl and add the tomatoes, olives and feta.
3. Finally, drizzle a good glug of olive oil over everything, season generously with salt and pepper, then toss together. That's it.

Sticky Peach & Goat's Cheese Salad

Serves 4

This is a heavenly combination: sweet, soft peaches, creamy and salty goat's cheese, crunchy hazelnuts and tart balsamic – it just works!

- 2 handfuls of mixed salad leaves or shredded lettuce
- 3 peaches, destoned and sliced
- 100g (3½oz) goat's cheese
- 1 handful of chopped hazelnuts
- good drizzle of balsamic glaze

1 Lay the salad leaves across a serving plate.

2 Top with the peach slices and arrange slices of goat's cheese around the peaches.

3 Sprinkle over the hazelnuts, then drizzle over the balsamic glaze. Season with salt and pepper if you wish, and that's it!

Quick Dinners

Cheesy Cajun Chicken

Frying Pan

Serves 4

This is a perfect dinner to make when you haven't got a lot of time. I usually just plonk the whole pan down in the middle of the table with some tortilla wraps, and perhaps some sliced avocado, and let everyone sort themselves out.

- 2–3 skinless and boneless chicken breasts, cut into strips
- 2 tbsp Cajun seasoning
- 6 salad tomatoes, quartered
- 300g (11oz) mixed peppers, deseeded and sliced (fresh or frozen)
- 1 handful of grated Cheddar

FOR COOKING
sunflower oil

1. Add the chicken and Cajun seasoning to a large frying pan with a drizzle of oil over a medium heat. Mix to coat the chicken, then fry until golden on the outside.

2. Add the tomatoes and mixed peppers and turn the heat down to low. Bring everything to a simmer, stirring regularly, using a spoon to partly squash the tomatoes so they form a sauce.

3. Remove from the heat, season if you wish and sprinkle over the grated cheese. Leave to stand for a few minutes, allowing the cheese to melt, then serve up!

Sticky Prawn Noodles

Serves 4

The key to making this taste genuinely authentic is to let the pan get really hot before adding the sauce. This will give the dish an extra smokiness, which is what makes a Chinese takeaway smell so inviting!

- 225g (8oz) raw prawns
- 2 onions, roughly chopped
- 1 green pepper, deseeded and cut into thick strips
- 300g (11oz) straight-to-wok udon noodles
- 4 tbsp hoisin sauce

FOR COOKING
sunflower oil

1. Add the prawns with a little oil to a frying pan over a high heat. Fry until pink and crispy, then remove from the pan.
2. Add the onions and pepper to the pan and fry until starting to colour.
3. Return the prawns and noodles to the pan, stirring regularly to ensure everything gets very hot – it should be almost catching on the bottom of the pan.
4. Remove from the heat, add the hoisin sauce with a splash of cold water and give it a good stir. Season if you wish, then serve!

BBQ Bean Burgers

Frying Pan

Vegetarian

Serves 4

A lot of veggie burgers are made with what I call 'filler'. This is usually flour or breadcrumbs, and while this is absolutely fine, they always leave me wanting more than one! These ones are super filling and packed with good protein, thanks to the butter beans. They're also a great way of making one tin of humble beans into a meal for the whole family. We usually have them as conventional burgers (served in a bun) with some chips and extra BBQ sauce for dipping. You could also toss in some salad leaves to get that veg count in.

- 1 x 400g (14oz) tin of butter beans, drained
- 1 red onion, finely diced
- 1 handful of grated red Leicester, plus a little extra to serve
- 1 egg
- 2 tbsp BBQ sauce

FOR COOKING

- sunflower oil

1. Using the back of a fork, mash the butter beans on a plate until they have broken down and formed a thick paste. Add to a large bowl with the red onion and cheese.
2. Crack the egg into the mixture, give it a very good mix and, using wet hands, mould the mixture into 4 burger shapes.
3. Add the burger patties with a drizzle of oil to a large frying pan over a medium heat. Fry on both sides until golden and crispy.
4. Using a pastry brush, brush the burgers on both sides with the BBQ sauce and top with a little grated cheese.
5. Turn the heat off, add a couple of tablespoons of cold water to the pan and place a lid or sheet of foil over the top to allow the cheese to melt. You're ready to serve!

Sweet Chilli Salmon with Rice

Serves 4

This is one of my go-to recipes when I want something quick and healthy (or if I've suddenly realised the salmon in my fridge is going to be out of date if we don't eat it right now). Sweet, sticky salmon, slightly charred, bitter broccoli, and rice that picks up all of the above flavours – yum!

- 1 handful of tenderstem broccoli, sliced
- 2 x 225g (8oz) packets of microwave rice
- 2 tbsp soy sauce
- 4 skin-on salmon fillets
- 4 tbsp sweet chilli sauce

FOR COOKING
- sunflower oil

1 Add the broccoli and some oil to a large, hot frying pan and cook until it's starting to crisp up. Add the rice and cook until piping hot. Take off the heat and add the soy sauce along with 2 tablespoons of water. Mix thoroughly, allowing the liquid to deglaze the pan, then tip the mixture onto plates.

2 Rinse out your pan and pop it back over a medium heat. Add a drizzle of oil then add the salmon fillets, skin-side down. Fry for a couple of minutes, or until the skin is crispy enough to slide a spatula underneath, then remove them from the pan. Place a piece of baking parchment in the pan and place the salmon fillets, skin-side up, on the parchment.

3 Drizzle the sweet chilli sauce over the top of each fillet and cook for 3–4 minutes. Check one to see if it is cooked through, then serve on top of the rice and broccoli.

Mediterranean Cod & Lentils with Olive Salsa

Traybake

Serves 4

This meal just makes me happy. It's such a fantastic, sunny combination of flavours, and even better if you keep the olives in the fridge – cold salsa with hot tomatoey lentils and fish is such a delicious mixture.

- 2 x 400g (14oz) tins of lentils, drained
- 2 cups (500ml/18fl oz) passata
- 2 handfuls of pitted mixed olives
- 3–4 cod fillets
- 1 handful of basil leaves

FOR COOKING & THE SALSA
olive oil

1 Preheat the oven to 220°C (200°C fan).

2 Add the lentils, passata and half the olives to an ovenproof dish. Season, give it a good mix, then bake in the hot oven for 15 minutes.

3 Remove the dish from the oven and add the cod fillets, skin-side up. Drizzle a little olive oil over the top of the fish and bake for 25 minutes.

4 Meanwhile, finely slice the remaining olives and the basil and add them to a bowl along with a good drizzle of olive oil. Season with salt and pepper and mix thoroughly.

5 Once the fish is cooked, remove the dish from the oven and spoon over the olive and basil salsa. You're ready to serve!

Honey Mustard Roast Salmon with Chips

Serves 4

Fish and chips, but fancier and a lot healthier! Sticky, sweet salmon and broccoli with crispy chips all done in the same tray. It's simple and delicious done well.

- frozen oven chips (as many as you think you'll eat)
- 4 salmon fillets
- 2 tbsp wholegrain mustard
- 2 tbsp honey
- 2 handfuls of tenderstem broccoli

FOR COOKING
- sunflower oil

1. Preheat the oven to 220°C (200°C fan).
2. Place the oven chips in a large tray and cook in the oven according to the packet instructions.
3. Meanwhile, cut out 4 squares of baking parchment and place one fillet of salmon on each one, skin-side up.
4. In a small bowl, mix the mustard and honey. Once the chips have had their time in the oven, place the salmon fillets on their parchment squares in the same tray. Add a little of the honey and mustard dressing to the skin of each one.
5. Add the broccoli to the tray with a little oil and return the whole lot to the oven for 12 minutes.
6. Remove from the oven and check the salmon is cooked to your liking, then spoon the remaining dressing over the broccoli and chips. Remove the salmon from the parchment and serve.

Gochujang Salmon with Hot Potato Salad

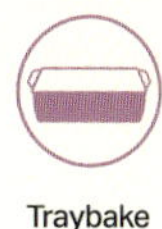

Serves 4

This is a perfect fuss-free midweek meal that looks and sounds like it was quite a faff to make, but really wasn't!

- 500g (1lb 2oz) new potatoes
- 2 tbsp gochujang paste
- 2 tbsp mayonnaise
- 4 salmon fillets
- 1 cup (160g/5½oz) edamame beans

FOR COOKING
- sunflower oil

1. Preheat the oven to 200°C (180°C fan).
2. Add the potatoes to a large roasting tray with a good drizzle of oil and some seasoning and bake for 30 minutes.
3. Meanwhile, in a bowl, combine the gochujang, mayonnaise and 2 tablespoons of boiling water to loosen it, and mix to form a sauce.
4. Add the salmon fillets to the potatoes and brush a little of the sauce over each fillet.
5. Bake for 12 minutes until the salmon is cooked, then remove from the oven and use a fork to break the salmon apart into large, flaky chunks. Tip both the potatoes and salmon onto a large plate or bowl.
6. Pop the edamame beans into a lidded container with a splash of cold water and microwave on high for 2 minutes. Drain, then scatter across the potatoes and salmon.
7. Finally, drizzle the remaining sauce over the top of everything and tuck in!

Roasted Sausage & Lentil Brie Bake

Traybake

Serves 4

Roasting Brie is something I've only started doing in the last couple of years, and frankly I'm cross it's taken me so long to discover it! Salty, creamy melted cheese, sweet, sticky sausages and garlicky lentils make perfect one-pot comfort food.

- 1 x 400g (14oz) tin of lentils, drained
- 2 red onions, roughly chopped
- 2 garlic cloves, finely chopped
- 100g (3½oz) Brie, cut into cubes
- 6–8 sausages

FOR COOKING
sunflower oil

1 Preheat the oven to 200°C (180°C fan).

2 In a large ovenproof dish, combine the lentils, onions, garlic and Brie, along with a drizzle of oil, and mix thoroughly.

3 Place the sausages on top and bake for 40 minutes, stirring halfway, until the sausages are browned and cooked, then remove and you're ready to serve!

Sundried Tomato Orzotto

Serves 4

Simple, honest flavours, and the sauce tastes better than anything ready-made you can buy in a jar!

- 1 x 400g (14oz) tin of chopped tomatoes
- 1 cup (200g/7oz) orzo
- 1 x 285g (10oz) jar of sundried tomatoes
- 1 handful of grated Parmesan
- 1 bunch of basil, leaves only

1. Add the chopped tomatoes, orzo and a handful of the sundried tomatoes, cut into strips, to a large saucepan. Fill the chopped tomato tin with water and add that too. Give it a good mix and allow it to simmer over a low heat until the orzo is soft, stirring occasionally.

2. While the orzo is cooking, add the remaining sundried tomatoes, the Parmesan and a good glug of the oil from the tomato jar to a blender and blitz to a paste.

3. Once the orzo is cooked, stir the paste and basil leaves through the orzo until combined, then serve!

Pea Green Gnocchi with Crispy Bacon

Serves 4

A classic combination of crispy bacon, peas, cheese and potatoes (gnocchi), this can be whipped up in 15 minutes from start to finish. If you haven't tried frying your gnocchi before, this is your sign! They're like chips but better!

- 3–4 rashers of back bacon, finely diced
- 500g (1lb 2oz) gnocchi
- 1 handful of grated Parmesan, plus extra to garnish
- 2 cups (260g/9¼oz) defrosted peas
- 1 chicken stock cube

FOR COOKING
- sunflower oil

1. Start by adding the bacon with a drizzle of oil to a large frying pan over a high heat. Cook until the bacon is browned and crispy.
2. Use a spoon to remove the bacon, add the gnocchi to the same frying pan and turn the heat down to low. Gently move it around for 10 minutes or so, until it is golden and crispy on all sides. Return the bacon to the pan along with the Parmesan, stirring until everything is coated. Take off the heat.
3. Meanwhile, add the peas, stock cube and 80ml (2¾fl oz) boiling water to a food processor and blitz until smooth and creamy.
4. Combine the pea purée with the crispy gnocchi and bacon, sprinkle with Parmesan and serve!

Quick Comfort Chicken Casserole

Saucepan

Serves 4

This is a great way to stretch two or three chicken breasts across a whole meal and give everyone something wholesome and hearty for dinner.

- 1 onion, finely sliced
- 2–3 skinless and boneless chicken breasts, cut into chunks
- 1 cup (150g/5oz) frozen mixed veg
- 1 x 565g (1lb 4oz) tin of potatoes, drained
- 1 x 400g (14oz) tin of chicken soup

FOR COOKING
sunflower oil

1 Add the onion to a saucepan along with a little oil and sauté until golden but not crispy.

2 Add the chicken and cook for 5 minutes or so, until golden on all sides.

3 Add the mixed veg, potatoes and soup, then refill the soup tin with water and add that too. Give it all a good stir.

4 Bring everything to a simmer and cook for about 10 minutes, until it is gently bubbling and has reduced to a thickened mixture. Take a piece of chicken out to check it's cooked all the way through. Season if you wish and serve!

Thai Lentil Curry

Saucepan

Vegetarian

Serves 4

As quick and simple as it is delicious! This is so healthy it's ridiculous, and as speedy, comforting bowls of tasty food go, this ticks a lot of boxes. You can add many other ingredients to it – leftover roast chicken or some fried tofu would be lovely, as well as lots of additional veggies.

- 2 onions, finely sliced
- 2 heaped tbsp Thai green curry paste
- 2 x 400g (14oz) tins of lentils, drained
- 1 x 400g (14oz) tin of full-fat coconut milk
- 1 handful of mangetout

FOR COOKING
sunflower oil

1 Add the onions and a little oil to a large saucepan over a medium heat and cook for 5–10 minutes, until soft and translucent.

2 Add the curry paste and lentils and give everything a good mix. Turn the heat down to low and add the coconut milk and mangetout. Stir together.

3 Bring everything to a gentle simmer, check for seasoning, then you're ready to eat!

Creamy Spinach & Walnut Spaghetti

Serves 4

Comfort food, but seriously full of flavour and vitamins! This sauce is so good you'll probably wish you'd made more – you might even find you do what I do, which is to make a double batch of the sauce and freeze it for an even quicker dinner when you're due a food shop!

- 250g (9oz) spinach leaves
- 1 cup (125g/4½oz) walnuts
- 50g (1¾oz) grated Parmesan
- juice of 1 lemon wedge
- 250g (9oz) dried spaghetti

1. Add the spinach, along with 2 tablespoons of water, to a large saucepan over a medium heat. Pop the lid on for 2 minutes.
2. Remove the spinach and add it to a food processor with the walnuts, Parmesan and lemon juice. Don't blitz it just yet.
3. To the same saucepan, add the spaghetti along with enough boiling water to cover it, and cook according to the packet instructions, until tender. Drain, saving a little pasta cooking water, and return the spaghetti to the saucepan.
4. Add the reserved pasta water to the food processor, and blitz until smooth and silky.
5. Check the sauce for seasoning, then add it to the cooked spaghetti, mix thoroughly and gently heat through. You're ready to eat!

Speedy Cashew, Broccoli & Coconut Curry

Serves 4

Cashews in a curry are my new favourite thing! They soften slightly but hold their shape and add a lovely rich, sweet toastiness to anything you cook them in.

- 2 red onions, finely sliced
- 1 cup (125g/4½oz) cashews
- 2 handfuls of chopped broccoli
- 70g (2½oz) curry paste (any sort)
- 1 x 400g (14oz) tin of full-fat coconut milk

FOR COOKING
sunflower oil

1 Add the onions and a little oil to a saucepan over a medium heat and fry for about 5 minutes, until soft and translucent. Add the cashews and toast them until starting to turn golden.

2 Turn the heat down to low and add the broccoli and curry paste. Give it a good stir so everything is coated, and pour in the coconut milk. Stir again.

3 Simmer gently for about 10 minutes, allowing the curry to thicken and reduce. Check for seasoning and you're ready to eat.

Cheesy Lentil & Bean Chilli

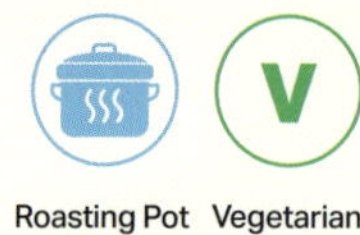

Serves 4

This is incredibly budget-friendly while being very delicious and filling. I usually serve it with rice and a little salad, but you could serve it in bowls with a hunk of bread, with some green beans on the side, or wrapped in tortillas with crunchy lettuce and extra cheese – yum!

- 1 x 400g (14oz) tin of lentils, drained
- 1 x 400g (14oz) tin of mixed beans in spiced sauce
- 1 x 400g (14oz) tin of chopped tomatoes
- 50g (1¾oz) chilli con carne seasoning
- 1 handful of grated Cheddar/red Leicester

1. Preheat the oven to 200°C (180°C fan).
2. Add the lentils, beans, tomatoes and chilli seasoning to a large roasting pot and mix thoroughly. Season generously, then place the lid on and bake for 45 minutes.
3. Remove from the oven, sprinkle the grated cheese across the top, pop the lid back on and allow to sit for 5 minutes for the cheese to melt. Then you're ready to eat!

Salt & Pepper Tofu Jumble

Serves 4

This is just like the takeaway version – except slightly healthier, much cheaper and, in my opinion, way more delicious!

- frozen oven chips (as many as you think you'll eat)
- 300g (11oz) firm tofu, cut into about 2cm (¾ inch) cubes
- 2 tbsp cornflour
- 2 peppers (ideally 1 green and 1 red), deseeded and sliced
- 1 x 35g (1¼oz) sachet of salt and pepper seasoning

FOR COOKING
sunflower oil

1. Add the chips with a little oil to your air fryer. Cook at 200°C for 15 minutes, tossing them halfway.

2. Meanwhile, put the tofu in a bowl with the cornflour and toss to coat. When the chips have had 15 minutes, add the tofu and air-fry for 10 minutes.

3. Add the peppers and salt and pepper seasoning, give everything a good mix and air-fry for a further 15 minutes, until the chips are golden and crispy. Remove and enjoy!

Cheesy Stuffed Meatballs with Country-style Potatoes

Serves 4

Rustic and delicious, this is a really filling meal that comes together in no time. Crispy potatoes, cheesy meatballs and baked tomato sauce – everyone's favourite things! You can also serve with a side of salad.

- 750g (1lb 10½oz) mini potatoes, halved
- 500g (1lb 2oz) pork mince
- 1 egg
- 100g (3½oz) soft mozzarella
- 500g (1lb 2oz) passata

FOR COOKING
- sunflower oil

1 Add the potatoes to the air fryer with a good drizzle of oil and cook at 200°C for 10 minutes, until golden and crispy, then remove.

2 Meanwhile, in a bowl, combine the pork mince with the egg and some seasoning, and mix thoroughly. Using wet hands, roll the mince into 18–20 balls and use your thumb to push a small chunk of mozzarella into the centre of each one.

3 Add the meatballs to the air fryer and cook for 10 minutes, then return the potatoes to the air fryer, pour the passata over everything and give it a good mix. Air-fry for a further 10 minutes, and then you're ready to eat.

Spiced King Prawn & Leek Risotto

Serves 4

This tastes like something you'd get in a good restaurant – I promise you!

170g (6oz) raw king prawns

2 tbsp harissa paste

1 cup (190g/6¾oz) arborio rice

1 leek, sliced

1 handful of grated Parmesan, plus extra to garnish

FOR COOKING
sunflower oil

1 Boil a kettle full of water before you start so you have hot water ready for the rice.

2 Add the prawns, along with a drizzle of oil and 1 tablespoon of the harissa paste, to a large saucepan over a high heat and fry until golden and crispy. Using a spoon, remove from the saucepan.

3 Add the rice to the same saucepan and toast it for a few minutes, before slowly adding the water a little at a time. Stir regularly and wait for the water to be absorbed by the rice before adding more water. It should take 15–20 minutes to fully cook the rice. About halfway through, add the leek.

4 Once the rice is fully cooked, return the prawns to the pan, along with the remaining harissa and the Parmesan.

5 Give it a good mix, sprinkle over some extra Parmesan and you're ready to eat!

Swedish Frankfurter Stew

Serves 4

Now, I know what you're thinking… frankfurters and stew? Is this a typo? No. It's actually a very popular dish in Scandinavian countries and it's delicious! This is the perfect recipe for when you haven't really got a lot of food in the house, or perhaps you're waiting for payday and need something to fill tummies without breaking the bank!

- 1 red onion, finely diced
- 6 frankfurter sausages, sliced into rounds
- 1 tbsp smoked paprika
- 1 x 400g (14oz) tin of chopped tomatoes
- 100ml (3½fl oz) single cream

FOR COOKING
- sunflower oil

1. Add the onion and sliced sausages to a large saucepan over a medium heat, along with a drizzle of oil and the smoked paprika. Fry for about 5 minutes, until both are starting to crisp up.
2. Add the chopped tomatoes and turn the heat down to low.
3. Bring everything to a simmer and, once gently bubbling, stir in the cream and leave to heat through for a further couple of minutes.
4. Season if you wish and serve!

Cauliflower Cheese Pasta

Serves 4

Rich, creamy cauliflower cheese with pasta – this simple crowd-pleaser tastes just as good cold the next day as it does freshly made.

- 400g (14oz) cauliflower florets
- 100ml (3½fl oz) single cream
- 1 heaped tbsp wholegrain mustard
- 250g (9oz) dried pasta
- 1 handful of grated Cheddar

1 Add the cauliflower to a large saucepan, cover with boiling water and boil for 5–10 minutes, until soft. Using a slotted spoon, remove it from the pan and add to a food processor, along with the cream and mustard. Don't blitz it up just yet.

2 Add the pasta to the cauliflower water and cook until tender, then drain, reserving a little pasta cooking water. Return the drained pasta to the saucepan.

3 Add the reserved pasta water to the food processor and blitz the cauliflower mixture until silky-smooth. Check for seasoning, then add the sauce to the cooked pasta along with the grated Cheddar.

4 Mix thoroughly, gently heat through, then spoon into bowls to serve.

Parma Ham Chicken Kyivs

Serves 4

This really is a whole plate of food cooked in the air fryer: gorgeous cheesy chicken Kyivs wrapped in crispy Parma ham, with crunchy chips and sweet asparagus.

- 4 skinless and boneless chicken breasts
- 4 tbsp garlic roule/ Boursin cheese
- 8 slices of Parma ham
- frozen oven chips (as many as you think you'll eat)
- 250g (9oz) asparagus spears

1 Butterfly the chicken breasts by holding them one at a time on a board with one hand and slicing horizontally through them until just before you reach the other side, to create a pocket. Stuff a tablespoon of garlic roule cheese into each pocket. Wrap 2 slices of Parma ham around each breast, trying to ensure they are sealed as well as you can.

2 Air-fry the chicken and the chips at 200°C for 20 minutes, adding the asparagus for the last 5 minutes. If your air fryer is not big enough to cook them together, start with the chips and remove, then cook the chicken, adding the asparagus for the last 5 minutes. Give the chips a final 2 minutes in the air fryer while you are plating the chicken and asparagus.

OPINEL
INOX

Sticky Miso Aubergine with Rice

Serves 4

Miso and aubergine were meant to know each other. Aubergine goes all soft, sweet and smoky when air-fried or roasted, and covering it with an umami miso dressing brings out even more of those lovely flavours!

- 2 aubergines
- 1 tbsp miso paste
- 1 tbsp honey
- 3 tbsp sesame oil
- 2 x 250g (9oz) packets of microwave rice

1. Slice the aubergines in half lengthways and score the flesh in diagonal criss-cross lines. You can cut deeply as long as you don't cut as far as the skin.

2. In a small bowl, combine the miso, honey and sesame oil.

3. Place the aubergine halves, skin-side down, in the air fryer. Use a pastry brush to coat the scored flesh with some of the miso dressing.

4. Air-fry at 200°C for 10 minutes, then brush more dressing over them and cook for a further 10 minutes. After 5 minutes, add the rice to cook in the aubergine juices and dressing.

5. Spoon the rice into bowls and top with the sticky aubergine halves. If you have any dressing left over, drizzle it over the top.

Melt-in-the-Middle Vegetarian Bake

Traybake

Vegetarian

Serves 4

Melted feta pasta had its moment and this is a similar concept, but even more delicious, in my opinion – not to mention that it's a great way to use up old vegetables and give them a new lease of (cheesy, garlicky) life!

150g (5oz) garlic roule/ Boursin cheese

2 sweet potatoes, cut into about 2cm (¾ inch) cubes (unpeeled)

2 peppers (red, yellow or orange), deseeded and chopped

2 red onions, finely sliced

1 large handful of spinach leaves

FOR COOKING
sunflower oil

1. Preheat the oven to 200°C (180°C fan).
2. Place the cheese in the centre of an ovenproof dish. Scatter the sweet potatoes, peppers and onions around it, drizzle a little oil over the top of the vegetables and bake for 1 hour, until all the veg are cooked.
3. Remove from the oven, add the spinach and a few tablespoons of water and give everything a good mix so the melted cheese mixes with all the vegetables and the spinach steams and wilts in the hot vegetables.
4. You're ready to eat!

Leek, Chorizo & Asparagus Orzotto

Serves 4

This tastes like a lot more ingredients went into it than did, with fried chorizo accounting for the lion's share of flavour. Sweet leeks, salty and smoky chorizo, fresh woody asparagus and creamy pasta – what's not to love?

- 100g chorizo, finely sliced
- 1 leek, finely sliced
- 1 cup (200g/7oz) orzo
- 100g (3½oz) asparagus spears, sliced
- 80g (2¾oz) cream cheese

FOR COOKING
sunflower oil

1 Add the chorizo with a little oil to a saucepan over a high heat and fry until crispy, then add the leek and sauté until soft.

2 Add the orzo along with 2 cups (500ml/18fl oz) boiling water and the asparagus, give it a good stir and turn the heat down to low. Cook, stirring occasionally to prevent it from sticking, until the orzo is soft, then take off the heat and add the cream cheese.

3 Give everything a good mix, check for seasoning and you're ready to serve!

Thai Green Butter Bean Curry

Serves 4

This is a great meal to have in your arsenal when you've not got a lot of food in the house but want something warming and full of flavour.

- 1 x 400g (14oz) tin of butter beans
- 3 tbsp Thai green curry paste
- 1 x 400g (14oz) tin of full-fat coconut milk
- 2 red onions, sliced
- 2 handfuls of spinach leaves

1. Preheat the oven to 200°C (180°C fan).
2. Add everything except the spinach to a roasting pot. Season and mix thoroughly, then cook in the oven for 45 minutes.
3. Remove from the oven, add the spinach, and pop the lid back on to allow the spinach to steam for a few minutes.
4. Stir and serve!

Slow and Simple

Crispy Chicken & Leek with Parmesan Beans

Serves 4

This is proper comfort food: filling, delicious and easy to make. It's something I make often, usually with a green salad, and the smells of roasting chicken, rosemary and Parmesan is a quick way to get everyone assembled in the kitchen ready to eat!

- 1 x 400g (14oz) tin of cannellini beans, drained
- leaves from 1 sprig of rosemary
- 2 handfuls of grated Parmesan
- 1 leek, finely diced
- 4–6 skin-on, bone-in chicken thighs

FOR COOKING
sunflower oil

1. Preheat the oven to 200°C (180°C fan).
2. Add the beans, rosemary, half the Parmesan and the leek to an ovenproof dish, then give it a good mix together with a little oil.
3. Place the chicken thighs on top, skin-side up, sprinkle the remaining Parmesan over the chicken and season everything.
4. Bake in the oven for 1 hour, until the chicken skin is golden and crispy, then remove and serve.

Hunter's Chicken Gnocchi

Serves 4

This is one of those meals to cheer you up at the end of a bad day. Perhaps you made a mistake at work, got stuck in traffic, spilt coffee all over yourself on the way into an important meeting, or perhaps your kids are testing your limits. Whatever the scenario, this is bound to turn your day around. Cheesy gnocchi and chicken with a rich tomatoey BBQ sauce bubbling away – it smells amazing and it tastes even better.

- 2–3 skinless and boneless chicken breasts, cut into chunks
- 500g (1lb 2oz) gnocchi
- 2 x 400g (14oz) tins of chopped tomatoes
- 100ml (3½fl oz) BBQ sauce
- 2 handfuls of grated Cheddar

1. Preheat the oven to 220°C (200°C fan).
2. Add the chicken, gnocchi, chopped tomatoes and BBQ sauce to a large ovenproof dish and mix thoroughly.
3. Scatter the grated cheese across the top and bake for 1 hour, until the chicken is cooked and the sauce is nice and rich. Remove, and you're ready to serve!

Italian Lemon Chicken

Traybake

Serves 4

This is so simple to make and tastes as though a lot more effort went into it than it did! Lovely on a warm summer's evening, enjoyed in the garden with a glass of cold white wine. Heaven.

- 500g (1lb 2oz) new potatoes
- 1 courgette, roughly chopped
- 1 handful of pitted green olives
- 4–6 boneless skin-on chicken thighs
- ½ lemon

FOR COOKING
sunflower oil

1 Preheat the oven to 200°C (180°C fan).

2 Add everything except the lemon to an ovenproof dish, along with a good drizzle of oil, season generously and give it a good mix.

3 Squeeze lemon juice over the top then chop the squeezed-out half into pieces and nestle it among the other ingredients.

4 Cook for 1 hour, giving it all a good tumble halfway through. Serve, spooning any remaining juices from the dish over the top.

Roasted Aubergine Lasagne

Traybake

Vegetarian

Serves 4

This is precisely as delicious as it sounds! Aubergines take on a lovely smoky flavour when roasted. Combined with tangy cheese and sweet tomatoes, this really is everything you want from a lasagne – minus all the faffing around with other pans and extra processes.

2 aubergines, roughly chopped

500g (1lb 2oz) passata

250g (9oz) ricotta

2 handfuls of grated Cheddar

6–8 sheets of fresh lasagne

FOR COOKING
sunflower oil

1 Preheat the oven to 200°C (180°C fan).

2 Add the aubergine chunks to a large ovenproof dish (20cm x 30cm x 5cm), drizzle with oil, sprinkle with salt and roast for 30 minutes.

3 Remove from the oven, tip into a large bowl and partially mash with a fork. Add the passata to the aubergine and mix.

4 In another bowl, combine the ricotta and grated cheese, season if you wish, and mix thoroughly.

5 Then, in the ovenproof dish, layer the tomato and aubergine mixture, followed by 1 or 2 lasagne sheets, followed by the cheese mixture, and so on, until you reach the top, finishing with a layer of cheese mixture.

6 Return the dish to the oven for 25 minutes, until golden on top, then leave to stand for 5 minutes before slicing and serving!

Hasselback Halloumi Stuffed Aubergines

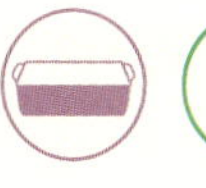
Traybake

Vegetarian

Serves 4

This might sound a little unusual but it's delicious and looks quite impressive once garnished. It's also very simple to make and full of complementary flavours.

- 2 aubergines, halved lengthways
- 1 x 225g (8oz) block of halloumi
- 1 cup (180g/6½oz) couscous
- 1 cup (160g/5½oz) pomegranate seeds
- 1 bunch of mint, leaves only, torn

FOR COOKING AND TO FINISH
olive oil

1. Preheat the oven to 200°C (180°C fan).
2. Add the aubergine halves, flesh-side up, to an oven tray and drizzle generously with olive oil. Bake for 30 minutes, then remove from the oven and gently flip them over. Use a knife to score deep lines into the soft skin, making sure not to cut all the way through.
3. Cut thin slices of halloumi from the block and slot them into each cut you've made, reserving the remaining block of halloumi.
4. Scatter the couscous around the aubergines into all the gaps. Pour 1 cup (250ml/8fl oz) boiling water over the couscous.
5. Grate the remaining halloumi across everything and return to the oven for 20 minutes, until the halloumi is golden and crispy.
6. Remove from the oven, scatter with the pomegranate seeds and top with torn mint leaves. Season and drizzle a little olive oil across the top and you're ready to eat!

Prawn Saag

Slow Cooker

Serves 4

Packed full of goodness and flavour, this is a lovely thing to walk through the door and smell on a cold day!

- 500g (1lb 2oz) frozen spinach
- 1 cup (130g/4½oz) defrosted frozen peas
- 30g (1oz) curry paste
- 1 x 400g (14oz) tin of full-fat coconut milk
- 200g (7oz) frozen raw prawns

1. Add the spinach, half the peas, the curry paste and coconut milk to the slow cooker and cook on high for 4 hours.
2. Add the prawns and the remaining peas, placing a tea towel between the pot and the lid, and cook for a further 1 hour.
3. Season to taste and serve!

Beef Goulash

Slow Cooker

Serves 4

Goulash always makes me think of mountains and snow. It's a delicious, smoky, hearty stew which is usually served in a chunky bowl with a doorstop wedge of bread and a spoon! Simple and perfect after a day outside in the cold.

- 500g (1lb 2oz) stewing beef, cut into chunks
- 1 x 400 (14oz) tin of chopped tomatoes
- 1 tbsp smoked paprika
- 2 red peppers, deseeded and sliced
- 2 cups (500ml/18fl oz) beef stock

1 Add all the ingredients to the slow cooker and cook on high for 6 hours, or until the beef is tender.

2 Check the seasoning, then spoon into bowls and enjoy!

Creamy Pepper Ravioli with Crispy Parmesan Chicken

Saucepan

Serves 4

This is one of those meals where you're best to just plonk the whole pan on the table and let people help themselves. Why? Because it's so delicious that there will be 'is there any more' requests and it saves you walking back and forth across the kitchen!

- 250g (9oz) ready-made fresh ravioli (filling of your choice)
- 2 x 280g (10oz) jars of peppers in oil
- 2–3 skinless and boneless chicken breasts, chopped into chunks
- 1 handful of grated Parmesan, plus extra to garnish
- 2–3 sprigs of basil, leaves only

1. Add the ravioli to a large saucepan, cover with boiling water and cook according to the packet instructions. Drain, reserving a little pasta cooking water, and set aside.

2. Add a few tablespoons of the oil from a pepper jar to the saucepan, along with the chicken, and fry the chicken over a medium heat for 4–6 minutes or until golden on all sides and cooked through.

3. Meanwhile, drain the peppers from the remaining oil (keeping the oil for future dishes) and add them to a food processor along with the Parmesan, reserved pasta water and most of the basil. Blitz until smooth and creamy.

4. Pour the sauce over the chicken pieces and return the ravioli to the saucepan. Bring everything to a simmer, tear the remaining basil leaves across the top and sprinkle with extra Parmesan.

Sticky Moroccan Beef with Chickpeas

Serves 4

Unexpectedly, this is one of my son's favourite recipes in the entire book! I think it's because the prunes add a lovely rich, sweet flavour and the beef is melt-in-your-mouth soft.

- 450g (1lb) stewing beef, cut into chunks
- 1 x 290g (10oz) tin of pitted prunes in syrup
- 1 x 400g (14oz) tin of chickpeas, drained
- 2 tbsp harissa paste
- 2 lemons

1 Add the beef, prunes (including the syrup from the tin), chickpeas and harissa to the slow cooker. Squeeze in the juice from one of the lemons. Mix together and cook on high for 6 hours.

2 Season to your taste, cut the remaining lemon into wedges and serve with the beef.

Lemonade Chicken

Slow Cooker

Serves 4

The name might throw you, but not as much as the ingredients list might! This is something I tried at someone else's house and couldn't work out for the life of me what on earth the sauce was. When I asked, I thought they were joking, and when I asked for the ingredients, I nearly started laughing! It's one of those things that shouldn't work but very much does, and tastes almost like Chinese sticky chicken. Give it a go!!

- 4–6 skinless and boneless chicken thighs, sliced
- 1 cup (250ml/8fl oz) lemonade
- 175ml (6fl oz) ketchup
- 1 tbsp brown sugar
- 2 tbsp cornflour

1. Add the chicken, lemonade, ketchup and sugar to your slow cooker. Combine the cornflour with a splash of water in a small bowl and mix to form a paste. Add the mixture to the slow cooker and give everything a good stir, seasoning as you prefer.

2. Cook on high for 6 hours, then check the seasoning and that's it!

Black Bean Dahl

Serves 4

I don't know about you, but I go through food obsessions, where I'll find something I really like and eat it so much I can't have it again for a while because I've eaten almost nothing else for a few weeks. Well, introducing my black bean dhal which was, for a time, a deep food obsession. Tom usually puts a stop to my obsessions because he gets bored more quickly than I do, but there was about a month where, if you ate at my house, you'd be served a portion of this! It's so comforting, cheap, filling and delicious.

- 6–8 garlic cloves, finely sliced
- 1 tbsp cumin seeds
- 1 large onion, finely diced
- 2 x 400g (14oz) tins of black beans
- 2 tbsp butter

1. Add the garlic, cumin seeds and onion to your slow cooker. Drain one tin of black beans, then add the beans to the slow cooker, along with the beans and liquid from the second tin. Mix together.
2. Cook on high for 4 hours, then, using a stick blender, briefly dip the blender into the pot and break down some of the beans (with the aim of thickening the mixture, not puréeing the whole lot). Season to your preference.
3. Spoon into bowls and add a little knob of butter to the top of each serving, to melt and stir through the dhal.

Mango Chicken Curry

Slow Cooker

Serves 4

In the interests of full disclosure, I confess I have slightly stolen this idea from my friend (she knows I've done it, before you get worried). She made me a lovely chicken curry, and when she told me her secret ingredient was lashings of mango chutney IN the sauce, I was determined to make my own version! We often serve mango chutney on the side, but why shouldn't it be more central to the dish? It adds a lovely sweetness and depth to the overall flavour. Serve with naan for an especially hearty meal.

- 3 skinless and boneless chicken breasts, cut into chunks
- 1 tbsp garam masala
- 4 garlic cloves, chopped
- 1 x 400g (14oz) tin of chopped tomatoes
- 2 tbsp mango chutney, plus a little extra for serving

1. Add the chicken, garam masala, garlic and chopped tomatoes to your slow cooker and cook on high for 4 hours.
2. Add the mango chutney and give it a good mix.
3. Season if you wish and serve with a little dollop of extra mango chutney on the top.

Tuscan Chicken Stew

Serves 4

I love the flavours of Tuscan chicken, and this is an especially simple version for when you have time to make it in the slow cooker. Serve with some rocket to get your greens in.

- 1 x 285g (10oz) jar of sundried tomatoes in oil
- 3 skinless and boneless chicken breasts, cut into chunks
- 150ml (¼ pint) single cream
- few sprigs of basil, leaves only
- 1 handful of grated Parmesan

1. Add most of the sundried tomatoes (save 3 or 4 pieces and cut them into slices) to a food processor along with the oil from the jar and blitz until it forms a paste.
2. Add the chicken to your slow cooker along with the sundried tomato paste and the reserved sundried tomato strips.
3. Add 200ml (7fl oz) water and cook on high for 4 hours.
4. Add the cream, basil and half the Parmesan, mix together, then place a tea towel between the pot and the lid and cook for a further 10 minutes over a low heat, or until the Parmesan has melted and the cream is heated through. Avoid simmering, as this will cause the cream to split.
5. Finally, spoon into bowls and sprinkle over the remaining Parmesan and any leftover basil.

Mexican Chicken Tacos

Slow Cooker

Serves 4

If I'm having people over, I'll often make this. It's a delicious one to make in advance and pop on the table along with some tortillas and salad, then let people help themselves to however much or little they fancy.

- 4 skinless and boneless chicken breasts, cut into chunks
- 30g (1oz) sachet of taco seasoning
- 1 x 400g (14oz) tin of chopped tomatoes
- 2 peppers (red, yellow or orange), deseeded and sliced
- 1 handful of grated Cheddar

1. Add the chicken, taco seasoning, tomatoes and peppers to your slow cooker, mix together and cook on high for 4 hours.
2. Add the grated cheese, place a tea towel between the pot and lid and turn the heat off. Leave to stand for 10 minutes, or until the cheese has melted, then serve.

Peppercorn Beef

Slow Cooker

Serves 4

Don't be put off by the amount of peppercorns or, indeed, the fact they're left whole! They soften almost to the texture of lentils, and if you like a classic peppercorn sauce with your steak, this recipe is for you! It's rich, creamy and full of flavour, and I like to serve it with a generous dollop of creamy mashed potatoes.

- 400g (14oz) stewing beef, cut into chunks
- 1 beef stock cube
- 2 onions, sliced
- ¼ cup (30g/1oz) black peppercorns
- 100g (3½oz) cream cheese

1. Add the beef, stock cube, onions and peppercorns to your slow cooker, along with 175ml (6fl oz) boiling water. Cook on high for 6 hours, or until the beef is tender.

2. Add the cream cheese, mix thoroughly, place a tea towel between the pot and the lid and cook for a further 10–15 minutes before serving.

Chicken Sausage & Mushroom Stew

Serves 4

You won't find a simpler recipe to follow anywhere else! Comfort food achieved with virtually no effort whatsoever.

- 8 chicken sausages
- 2 red onions, sliced
- 1 x 400ml (14fl oz) tin of tomato soup
- 200g (7oz) baby chestnut mushrooms
- 1 sprig of thyme

1 Add everything to the slow cooker and cook on high for 4 hours.

2 Season if you wish and enjoy!

Triple Cheese Mac & Cheese

Serves 4

I actually don't think this needs introducing at all because it's got three types of cheese in it, which is already basically excellent if you like cheese. You could serve it with a salad on the side – or just enjoy the cheesy deliciousness as is.

- 300g (11oz) dried macaroni
- 600ml (20fl oz/1 pint) milk
- 1 cup (115g/4oz) grated Cheddar
- 1 cup (115g/4oz) grated mozzarella
- 1 cup (115g/4oz) grated red Leicester

1. Add all the ingredients to the slow cooker and cook on high for 4 hours or until the pasta is cooked, stirring occasionally.
2. Season with black pepper to taste, and that's it.

Cajun BBQ Pulled Pork Rolls

Slow Cooker

Serves 4

If you're hosting lots of people but don't want to be faffing and running around in the kitchen with silly little things on trays, make a pot of this. Then relax with a drink in your hand while everyone busies themselves making THEIR OWN plate of food. Ideal!

- 1kg (2¼lb) pork shoulder joint
- 3 tbsp Cajun seasoning
- 3 red onions
- ½ cup (120g/4oz) BBQ sauce
- 4 bread rolls

1. Add the pork coated with Cajun seasoning to your slow cooker. Slice 2 of the onions and add those too. Pour over enough water to cover everything, and cook on high for 8 hours.

2. Remove the pork joint and place it in a large bowl. Add the BBQ sauce and, using 2 forks, pull the meat apart into chunky shreds.

3. Slice the remaining onion.

4. Season the pulled pork to taste, then spoon into the rolls with a few slices of red onion added to each.

Harissa Chicken with Lemon, Apricot & Pearl Barley

Roasting Pot

Serves 4

This sounds so fancy and it looks so fancy and it is in fact quite fancy, but when you see the recipe you'll realise that it's incredibly easy to make. I did this for guests and placed it on a huge serving platter in the middle of the table. Everyone helped themselves and someone even asked if they could take a picture of it because it was so pretty! I'll often make extra dressing to serve on the side because it's just that good.

- 1 lemon, halved
- 1 cup (175g/6oz) pearl barley
- 1 cup (160g/5½oz) chopped dried apricots
- 1 medium chicken (about 1.5kg/3¼lb)
- 2 tbsp harissa paste

FOR COOKING
olive oil

1. Preheat the oven to 200°C (180°C fan).
2. Cut one lemon half into chunks and set the remaining half aside.
3. Add the pearl barley, dried apricots and lemon chunks to a roasting pot, then add 500ml (2 cups/18fl oz) water. Give it a good mix and a season then place the chicken on top.
4. In a bowl, combine the harissa with a good glug of olive oil and the juice from the remaining lemon half, and mix until it forms a dressing. Brush a little of the dressing mixture over the chicken skin, using a pastry brush or your hands.
5. Pop the lid on and roast for 1 hour, then remove the lid and return to the oven for a further 10 minutes. Remove from the oven, place the lid back on and leave to one side to steam for 15 minutes, then remove the chicken and carve into slices.
6. Spoon the barley mixture across a large platter or plates and place pieces of the cooked chicken on top. Drizzle any remaining dressing across the top and serve!

Spanish Aubergine Casserole

Serves 4

This is a perfect dump-and-run meal that tastes and smells like Spain. Perfect for a simple, no-fuss dinner! We usually have it in bowls, with crusty bread to get dunking.

- 1 handful of chopped chorizo
- 1 aubergine, finely chopped
- 1 x 400g (14oz) tin of chopped tomatoes
- 1 cup (120g/4oz) pitted black olives
- 1 x 400g (14oz) tin of cannellini beans, drained

1 Preheat the oven to 200°C (180°C fan).

2 Add all the ingredients to a roasting pot, then fill one of the empty tins with water and add that too. Season generously, stir to mix, and pop the lid on.

3 Bake in the oven for 1 hour, then remove the lid and bake for a further 10 minutes. That's it. Serve!

Cheesy Chicken & Chorizo Orzo

Roasting Pot

Serves 4

This is an all-round crowd pleaser. Think cheesy chicken and chorizo pasta, which most people enjoy already, but baked, which gives it an even greater depth of flavour.

- 1 cup (200g/7oz) orzo
- 1 handful of chopped chorizo
- 500g (1lb 2oz) passata
- 4–6 skinless and boneless chicken thighs
- 1 x 125 (4½oz) ball of mozzarella, torn

1. Preheat the oven to 200°C (180°C fan).
2. Add the orzo, chorizo and passata to a roasting pot along with 125ml (4fl oz) water and mix thoroughly. Top with the chicken thighs and season.
3. Place the lid on top and bake in the oven for 1 hour, then remove the lid and add the mozzarella across the top.
4. Return to the oven for 10 minutes, uncovered, then serve.

Slow-Cooked Lamb & Beans

Serves 4

Now, when I talk about roasting pots, I mean lidded dishes that go in the oven. But if you don't have one, no worries – just grab a deep oven dish, cover it tightly with foil, and follow the recipe as written. That's what I did here, mainly because it looked better! This might look like a slightly intimidating recipe, but it's as easy as it gets. Also, it smells INCREDIBLE when cooking, so your home will smell like a French bistro.

- ½ shoulder of lamb (about 1kg/2¼lb)
- 2 sprigs of thyme
- 2 x 400g (14oz) tins of butter beans, drained
- 2 large carrots, diced
- 3 onions, quartered

1. Preheat the oven to 200°C (180°C fan).
2. Add the lamb, thyme, butter beans, carrots and onions to a roasting pot. Add 1 litre (35fl oz/1¼ pints) water and season.
3. Pop the lid on and cook in the oven for at least 6 hours, checking after 4 hours that it hasn't dried out too much. If it has, top up with water.
4. Remove from the oven after 6 hours, and the meat should fall off the bone. Spoon the soupy beans onto a plate, followed by chunks of the lamb, and you're ready to eat.

Chicken & Cauliflower Peanut Butter Curry

Roasting Pot

Serves 4

When you put this in the oven uncooked, you'll wonder whether you've made a mistake, because it isn't one that feels like it's going to work. But once you've made it, you'll understand. Toasty cauliflower with chicken that's falling apart, all cooked in a lightly spiced, very rich, creamy curry sauce – it's perfect! I like a dollop of mango chutney on mine, and if you're really hungry this is delicious with the Golden Rice on page 205.

- 70g (2¾oz) curry paste (any sort)
- 4 tbsp peanut butter (I used smooth but crunchy works too!)
- 1 x 400g (14oz) tin of full-fat coconut milk
- 6 skinless and boneless chicken thighs
- 250g (9oz) cauliflower florets

1 Preheat the oven to 200°C (180°C fan).

2 Combine the curry paste, peanut butter and coconut milk in a jug and mix until combined.

3 Add the chicken and cauliflower to a roasting pot, followed by the sauce. Give everything a good mix, then pop the lid on and bake in the oven for 1 hour.

4 Remove the lid and bake for a further 10 minutes, to dry out slightly, before serving.

Cajun Halloumi Rice

Serves 4

A hug in a bowl! This is as comforting as it is delicious.

- 2 peppers (red, yellow or orange), deseeded and sliced
- 2 tbsp Cajun seasoning
- 1 cup (175g/6oz) basmati rice
- 1 x 400g (14oz) tin of chopped tomatoes
- 1 x 225g (8oz) block of halloumi, sliced

TO FINISH

- olive oil

1. Preheat the oven to 200°C (180°C fan).
2. Add the peppers, half the Cajun seasoning, the rice and tomatoes to a roasting pot. Fill the empty tomato tin with water and add this too. Season and mix thoroughly.
3. Pop the lid on, place the pot in the oven and bake for 45 minutes.
4. Remove the lid and add the halloumi slices across the top. Sprinkle the remaining Cajun seasoning across the halloumi and drizzle olive oil over the top.
5. Return the pot, uncovered, to the oven and bake for 15 minutes, before serving.

Soy Glazed Chicken & Noodles

Serves 4

This is one of Tom's favourite recipes from the book. The sweet, salty sauce goes all glossy and sticky, and coats the chicken and noodles like a dream!

- 100ml (3½fl oz) soy sauce
- 1 tbsp sugar
- 5 or 6 skinless and boneless chicken thighs
- 3 peppers (red, yellow or orange), deseeded and sliced
- 200g (7oz) dried vermicelli noodles

FOR COOKING
sunflower oil

1. Preheat the oven to 200°C (180°C fan).
2. In a small jug, combine the soy sauce and sugar and mix until the sugar has dissolved.
3. Add the chicken and peppers to a roasting pot, along with a little oil and half the sweet soy sauce mixture.
4. Pop the lid on and bake in the oven for 45 minutes.
5. Meanwhile, place the noodles in a heatproof bowl and cover with boiling water. Leave for 5 minutes (or until soft) then drain and set aside.
6. When the chicken has had its 45 minutes, add the cooked noodles plus the remaining soy mixture to the pot, mix thoroughly and return to the oven for 10 minutes. You're ready to eat!

Tarragon Chicken & Potatoes

Roasting Pot

Serves 4

This is a take on a lovely baked chicken and potato dish I had in the South of France. The original included a lot of double cream and butter, whereas this version is slightly lighter and healthier, albeit just as delicious.

- 6 skinless and boneless chicken thighs
- 2 tbsp dried tarragon
- 2 large potatoes (unpeeled), cut into about 2cm (¾ inch) cubes
- 300ml (10fl oz) crème fraîche
- 2 tbsp wholegrain mustard

FOR COOKING
sunflower oil

1. Preheat the oven to 200°C (180°C fan).
2. Add the chicken, tarragon and potatoes to a roasting pot along with a drizzle of oil and a generous pinch of seasoning. Mix together.
3. Pop the lid on and bake in the oven for 45 minutes. Add the crème fraîche and mustard and mix thoroughly. Return the pot, uncovered, to the oven for 10 minutes, then serve.

Sticky Chinese Chicken with Lemon

Serves 4

I have 'borrowed' this recipe from my mum! Sticky chicken with rice used to be one of my favourites, and the best bit is the last few spoonfuls of rice that have been sitting in the sweet, lemony sauce and have absorbed the most flavour. It's a 'lick the bowl clean' kind of situation.

- 1 lemon, halved
- 2 tbsp Chinese 5 spice
- 3 tbsp honey
- 3 onions, diced
- 6 skinless and boneless chicken thighs

FOR COOKING
- sunflower oil

1 Preheat the oven to 200°C (180°C fan).

2 Add the juice of one lemon half along with the remaining ingredients to the roasting pot. Add 1 tablespoon of oil and 250ml (1 cup/8fl oz) water, and mix thoroughly.

3 Place in the oven and bake for 45 minutes, then remove the lid and return to the oven for a further 15 minutes.

4 Serve with the remaining lemon half, cut into wedges.

Tortilla Soup

Serves 2

This sounds odd until you've tried it, and then it totally makes sense! The sliced tortillas turn the texture of chewy noodles and they soak up all the lovely flavours you've added.

- 1 cup (140g/4¾oz) sweetcorn, drained
- 1 x 400g (14oz) tin of black beans
- 1x 400g (14oz) tin of chopped tomatoes
- 1 x 30g (1oz) sachet of fajita seasoning
- 1 tortilla wrap

1 Add the sweetcorn, black beans (including the liquid from the tin), tomatoes and fajita seasoning to a slow cooker and cook on high for 4 hours.

2 Season if you wish, then turn the slow cooker off. Slice the tortilla into long, thin strips (like noodles or tagliatelle) and drop them into the soup. Mix and leave to soak for 10 minutes with the lid on, then serve!

Lamb Kofta Stew

Roasting Pot

Serves 4

This sounds like it would be a faff to make but it's seriously easy! All the lovely juices from the koftas melt into the potatoes, and the liquid from the tomatoes keeps the koftas soft and moist so they don't dry out. It works so well and is lovely served with a simple green salad.

- 500g (1lb 2oz) lamb mince
- 3 tbsp harissa paste
- 100g (3½oz) breadcrumbs
- 2 large potatoes (unpeeled), cut into about 1cm (½ inch) dice
- 2 x 400g (14oz) tins of chopped tomatoes

1. Preheat the oven to 220°C (200°C fan).
2. In a large bowl, combine the lamb mince, 1 tablespoon of the harissa and the breadcrumbs. Mix thoroughly then, using wet hands, form the mixture into 10–12 koftas.
3. Add the potatoes, tomatoes and remaining harissa to a roasting pot, season generously and mix well, then place the koftas on top.
4. Place the lid on the roasting pot then pop it in the oven and bake for 1 hour. Remove the lid and return the pot to the oven for 5–10 minutes to allow the koftas to crisp up a little (but no longer or they'll dry out).
5. Remove and you're ready to eat!

Sides and Snacks

Cheese & Onion Stuffed Sweet Potatoes

Serves 4

This is a really filling, cheap meal to make, and a great way to ensure you're getting a bit of goodness into everyone's dinner while knowing they'll actually eat it! Serve sweet potatoes and chickpeas on their own and there aren't many children (or perhaps adults) who'd scoff the lot, but combine them with two types of cheese and some spring onions and people will be asking for more!

- 4 sweet potatoes, halved lengthways
- ½ x 400g (14oz) tin of chickpeas, rinsed and drained
- 1 handful of grated Cheddar
- 4 spring onions, finely sliced
- 4 tbsp cream cheese

1. Place the sweet potatoes cut-side down in your air fryer and cook at 200°C for 20 minutes, until soft.
2. Remove and scoop the flesh out into a bowl, being careful not to tear the skins. Add the remaining ingredients to the bowl and mix.
3. Place the empty skins in the air fryer and scoop the filling mixture into each, packing in as much as possible.
4. Air-fry for a further 8 minutes, until golden and crispy. That's it!

Korean Halloumi Skewers

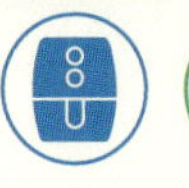

Air Fryer Vegetarian

Serves 4

Gochujang is something I always have a tub of in my fridge because it's cheap, delicious and a little goes a long way. Oh, and it goes so well with halloumi! We usually have these with a baked potato and a simple salad.

- 1 courgette, cut into large chunks
- 2 red peppers, deseeded and cut into large chunks
- 1 onion, cut into large chunks
- 200g (7oz) halloumi, cut into chunks
- 3 tbsp gochujang paste

FOR COOKING
sunflower oil

1. Place the courgette, peppers, onion and halloumi chunks in a bowl.
2. In a small bowl or jug, combine the gochujang paste with 1 tablespoon each of oil and boiling water. Mix to form a thick but pourable paste.
3. Pour the paste over the vegetables and halloumi and mix thoroughly. Thread everything onto skewers that will fit in your air fryer, and air-fry at 200°C for 10 minutes, until tender and caramelised on the outside. That's it!

Sort-of Caesar Salad

Serves 4

Yes, yes, yes: ready-made croûtons and shop-bought salad dressing. We're taking a few shortcuts here, but also we're fine with that because this is delicious and takes about two minutes to make from start to finish! Great for a quick, healthy lunch.

- 1–2 heads of lettuce, leaves separated
- 1 avocado
- 2 tbsp Caesar dressing
- 1 handful of ready-made croûtons
- 50g (1¾oz) Parmesan

1. Arrange the lettuce leaves on a large plate.
2. Slice the avocado in half, remove the stone and slice into chunks, dotting them across the leaves.
3. Drizzle over the dressing, then sprinkle over the croûtons.
4. Finally, using a swivel peeler, shave the Parmesan across the top. Dig in.

Vegan Japanese Broth

Saucepan

Vegan

Serves 4

Tom drinks this like you or I might drink a cup of tea – i.e. out of a mug! While I'm not suggesting you might like to try drinking this from a mug, you also might like to try drinking this from a mug?! The miso paste makes it very tasty and umami, and the ginger kick makes it feel very healthy. If you're feeling a bit under the weather, this is a great thing to whip up quickly and enjoy (from a mug or not)!

- 1 thumb-sized piece of ginger, peeled and grated
- 4 spring onions, finely sliced
- 1 tbsp white miso paste
- 1 vegetable stock cube
- 150g (5oz) silken tofu, cut into cubes

FOR COOKING
sunflower oil

1. Add the ginger and spring onions with a little oil to a large saucepan over a medium heat and fry for about 5 minutes, until the onions are starting to soften.
2. Add the miso paste along with 3 cups (750ml/1½ pints) boiling water and the stock cube, and leave to reduce for 10 minutes, stirring occasionally.
3. Finally, add the tofu, take off the heat and pop the lid on for a few minutes to allow the tofu to warm through. Don't stir as it is very delicate and will break apart.
4. Check for seasoning and serve!

Cabbage & Bacon with Creamy Butter Beans

Serves 4

I had this in Prague a few years ago on the insistence of the waitress who worked in the brewery we'd just toured around (and sampled quite a lot of). I didn't think it sounded very exciting but, being British, I politely agreed and also ordered myself a pork dish with mashed potato, thinking a bowl of cabbage wasn't going to satisfy me for lunch! What a mistake. Not only was the cabbage and bacon dish by far the best thing on the table, it was about the most filling and satisfying thing I've ever eaten! It's extremely cheap to make and is exactly the sort of thing to enjoy on a cold winter's evening with a chunk of crusty bread and a few pickled gherkins (no, really!)

- 3 rashers of back bacon, sliced into chunks
- ½ white cabbage, cut into thin strips
- 1 tbsp fennel seeds
- 1 x 400g (14oz) tin of butter beans
- 3 heaped tbsp cream cheese

FOR COOKING
sunflower oil

1. Add the bacon and a little oil to a hot frying pan and fry until crispy, then remove from the pan.
2. Add the cabbage and fennel seeds and fry until the cabbage is starting to turn crispy at the edges.
3. Add the butter beans, along with the liquid from their tin, turn the heat down to low and bring everything to a simmer.
4. Return the bacon to the pan along with the cream cheese, give everything a good stir and season if you wish. You're ready to serve!

Classic Egg Fried Rice

Frying Pan

Vegetarian

Serves 2

If you regularly order this from the takeaway, then you're going to love this recipe! If you want to achieve that authentic taste and smell, make sure the pan is really hot – so the rice is almost catching on the bottom – before adding the soy sauce.

- 2 eggs
- 4 spring onions, sliced
- 1 x 250g (9oz) packet of microwave rice
- 1 handful of beansprouts
- 2 tbsp soy sauce

FOR COOKING

- sunflower oil

1 Crack the eggs into a hot frying pan with a little oil. Fry over a high heat until cooked through, using a wooden spoon or spatula to break the egg down into chunks.

2 Add most of the spring onions (saving some to sprinkle over at the end) along with the rice and beansprouts and stir regularly, allowing everything to cook through and colour. Don't be afraid to let them catch; this smokiness adds to the flavour.

3 Finally, remove from the heat and add the soy sauce. Give it a final mix, sprinkle over the reserved spring onion and serve!

Italian Summer White Bean Salad

Serves 4

This is as uncomplicated as it gets! Delicious mopped up with a piece of warm crusty bread, or to accompany some steamed fish on a summer's day.

1 x 400g (14oz) tin of cannellini beans, rinsed and drained

½ red onion, finely sliced

½ lemon

1 handful of chopped parsley

FOR DRESSING
olive oil

1 Tip the beans and red onion into a large bowl.

2 Squeeze the lemon over the top and season with a little salt and pepper. Give it a good mix and then leave for 10 minutes to partly pickle the onions.

3 Add the parsley and olive oil, give it one final mix and you're ready to serve!

Pear & Walnut Salad with Blue Cheese

One Bowl

Vegetarian

Serves 4

This might not be everyone's cup of tea, but it's certainly mine! Not only does it look quite fancy (always an added bonus when you've only spent three minutes pulling something together) but it's like these five ingredients were actually made for each other!

- 1 chicory bulb (or other bitter salad variety), leaves separated
- 1 pear, finely sliced
- 50g (1¾oz) soft blue cheese, such as Gorgonzola
- 1 handful of crushed walnuts
- 2 tbsp honey

1. Arrange the chicory leaves across a large plate.
2. Add the pear slices on top and around the chicory.
3. Using a teaspoon, dot little amounts of the blue cheese around the plate.
4. Sprinkle the walnuts across the lot and drizzle the honey over the top to serve.

Mexican Stuffed Falafel

Air Fryer

Vegetarian

Serves 4

When you make falafel yourself, they're delicious and full of goodness. Not many people will attempt to make them from scratch because it sounds like a big faff for little reward, but these are surprisingly easy and come out almost like spicy, cheesy Scotch eggs! Great for picnics, lunchboxes or just something to snack on. I like a little mayonnaise on the side for dipping.

1 x 400g (14oz) tin of kidney beans, drained

30g (1oz) fajita seasoning

1 egg

½ cup (30g/1oz) breadcrumbs

100g (3½oz) soft mozzarella

FOR COOKING
oil spray

1 Add the kidney beans, fajita seasoning, egg and breadcrumbs to a food processor and blitz to a thick paste.

2 Using wet hands, roll the mixture into balls the size of golf balls (about 8) and use your thumb to push a chunk of mozzarella into the middle of each one.

3 Add the balls to your air fryer, spray with a small amount of oil and cook at 200°C for 15 minutes, gently turning them over halfway through so they cook evenly on all sides. Remove and enjoy!

Foolproof Tomato Salad

One Bowl

Vegetarian

Serves 4

Now, don't skip this recipe just because you think it looks like a boring plate of tomatoes with some greenery across the top. Unless you don't like tomatoes, in which case, maybe this one isn't for you, and fair enough. Garlicky, partly pickled sweet tomatoes with fresh herbs and lashings of good-quality olive oil – it's a winner!

500g (1lb 2oz) tomatoes, finely sliced into rounds

3 garlic cloves, minced

few basil leaves, roughly chopped

1 sprig of dill, roughly chopped

FOR DRESSING

olive oil

1 Arrange the tomato slices across a large plate. Season generously with salt and let sit for 20 minutes to partly pickle them.

2 Add the garlic to a jug along with the olive oil and a generous helping of black pepper. Whisk together.

3 Drizzle the garlic oil over the tomatoes and toss together, then sprinkle the chopped herbs over the top to serve.

Tom's Crunchy Pickled Cucumbers

Serves 4

Whatever we're eating, Tom will request something 'cold and crunchy' to accompany it. Be it Bolognese, a roast, a curry – you name it, his inner German feels that no meal is complete without it! This is something he makes in BULK and stores in large pickle jars in the fridge to have on hand for the next 3–4 weeks, and despite my first protestations that not every meal needs a pickled salad to go with it, I've somehow found myself also reaching for the jar!

- 1 red or white onion, finely sliced
- ½ cucumber, finely sliced
- 2–3 gherkins, finely diced (plus 4 tbsp pickling juice from the jar)
- 1 red chilli

1 Add everything to a large bowl, season generously with salt and give it a really good mix.

2 Cover the bowl with clingfilm and pop it in the fridge for at least 30 minutes, then drain off any liquid and serve!

Danish Kale Salad

One Bowl

Vegetarian

Serves 4

My sister-in-law introduced me to this salad about five years ago. She lives in Copenhagen and often makes a vast bowl of it and plonks it down in the middle of the table to accompany whatever else we're eating. To look at it, you might not be particularly excited to get stuck in, but it's delicious and somehow goes with everything. Bitter kale, sweet apple, salty feta, crunchy seeds and sticky balsamic: it works beautifully with roast chicken, grilled fish, slow-cooked meat, or to add some crunch to sandwiches!

- 1 bag (200g/7oz) chopped kale, stalks removed
- 2 apples, cored and finely diced
- 100g (3½oz) feta, crumbled
- 1 handful of mixed seeds
- drizzle of balsamic glaze

1. Add the kale to a large bowl and use scissors to chop it into smaller pieces.
2. Add the apple, feta and mixed seeds, then drizzle over the balsamic glaze and a little olive oil. Season generously and mix together.

Sesame Carrot Salad

One Bowl

Vegetarian

Serves 4

This goes with so many things, so make it in bulk and add a handful to anything you're serving to give it a tasty crunch. If you ever make chicken satay, this is something you need to serve alongside it! They pair perfectly.

- 3–4 carrots, peeled
- 2 tbsp sesame oil
- 1 tbsp soy sauce
- 1 tsp honey
- 1 tbsp sesame seeds

1 Using a swivel peeler, slice the carrots into ribbons then add them to a large bowl.

2 In a jug, combine the sesame oil, soy sauce, honey and sesame seeds. Whisk together to form a dressing, then pour over the carrot ribbons. Toss together, ensuring everything is coated, and you're done!

My Mum's Cheesy Leeks

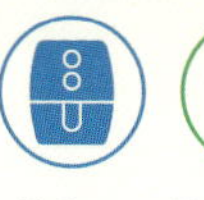
Air Fryer

Vegetarian

Serves 4

Cheesy baked veg is a staple when it comes to Sunday lunch and we usually alternate between cauliflower cheese and cheesy leeks. My mum always used to serve cheesy leeks with roast chicken and cauliflower cheese with roast beef – personally, I like both with both (maybe even at the same time!) but these mustardy, cheesy, sweet leeks are a meal in their own right, as well as the perfect accompaniment to a roast. Plus, the leftovers and crispy edge bits are yours to scoff or hide and eat later…

- 3 leeks, finely sliced
- 2 tbsp plain flour
- 300ml (10fl oz) double cream
- 1 tbsp Dijon mustard
- 1 cup (115g/4oz) grated Cheddar

FOR COOKING
sunflower oil

1 Add the leeks with a drizzle of oil to your air fryer and cook at 200°C for 5 minutes.

2 Sprinkle the flour across the leeks and give them a good stir. Add the cream and mustard, give everything another good mix, then top with the grated Cheddar. Air-fry for a further 15 minutes. That's it!

Spicy Cauliflower 'Wings' with Sriracha Mayo

Serves 4

Whenever cauliflower is positioned as a 'steak' or 'wings' or 'nuggets', people will say, 'I think we're expecting too much of cauliflower at this point'. But there's a reason we keep using cauliflower! It holds its shape, it's filling, it's delicious and it soaks up whatever flavour you cover it with like a sponge. Be warned: these cauliflower wings are VERY moreish, especially when dunked in that sauce. Yum!

- 4 tbsp cornflour
- 1 tbsp smoked paprika
- 1 cauliflower, cut into florets
- 5 tbsp mayonnaise
- 2 tbsp sriracha

FOR COOKING
oil spray

1 In a large bowl, combine the cornflour and smoked paprika along with some seasoning if you wish. Add ¼ cup (60ml/2fl oz) water and mix to form a thick batter.

2 Drop the cauliflower florets into the batter and turn to ensure they are fully coated.

3 Add the cauliflower to your air fryer, spray with oil, and cook at 200°C for 20 minutes, shuffling them around every 5 minutes to ensure maximum crispness.

4 Meanwhile, in a small bowl, combine the mayonnaise and sriracha (add more sriracha if you like it spicy) then get dipping with the cauliflower and enjoy!

Golden Rice

Serves 4

Baking rice has been a revelation to me. Not only is it a lot more forgiving (I think we've all made rice pudding that was accidentally crunchy with undercooked rice at least once in our lives) but it has a lovely toasty flavour to it when cooked in the oven. This is a beautiful dish and will definitely impress!

- 250g (9oz) basmati rice
- 600ml (20fl oz/1 pint) chicken stock
- 1 tsp ground turmeric
- 1 handful of flaked almonds
- 1 handful of pomegranate seeds

1. Preheat the oven to 200°C (180°C fan).
2. Combine the rice, stock, turmeric and flaked almonds in a roasting pot. Mix thoroughly, season as desired, then pop the lid on and bake in the oven for 45 minutes.
3. Remove from the oven and spoon the rice into a large bowl. Top with the pomegranate seeds and you're ready!

Thai Sweetcorn Fritters with Sweet Mango Dip

Makes 4

On their own these are delicious but, as is so often the case, the thing that really makes these sing is that sauce! It might sound like an odd combination, so you're going to have to trust me and try these for yourself!

- 1 cup (140g/5oz) sweetcorn
- 3 tbsp self-raising flour
- 2 tbsp Thai red curry paste
- 4 tbsp plain yoghurt
- 1 tsp mango chutney

FOR COOKING
sunflower oil

1. To a large bowl, add the sweetcorn, flour, 1 tablespoon of the curry paste and 2 tablespoons of water.
2. Mix thoroughly. Heat a little oil in a hot frying pan, then add tablespoon-sized amounts of the mixture.
3. Fry on both sides until golden and crispy, then pop them on a plate lined with kitchen towel to absorb any excess oil.
4. In a small bowl, combine the yoghurt, remaining tablespoon of curry paste and the mango chutney, and mix thoroughly. Get dipping!

Onion Bhajis

Frying Pan

Vegetarian

Makes 4

I love onion bhajis. They're delicious, so what's not to love? However, the idea of deep-fat frying anything hugely puts me off! It feels like a big waste of oil and, as someone who's had heart surgery twice in the last six years, I probably want to avoid too much deep-fat frying if I want to stay in my cardiologist's good books! These are considerably healthier, being shallow-fried, and you still get that fragrant, sweet, crispy onion flavour you're hoping for.

- 2 large onions, finely sliced
- 1 tbsp ground turmeric
- 1 tbsp chilli powder
- 6 tbsp cornflour
- ½ cup (110g/3¾oz) plain yoghurt

FOR COOKING

- sunflower oil

1. To a large bowl, add the onions, turmeric, chilli powder and cornflour, with a teaspoon of salt, and mix thoroughly until the onions are coated in the seasoning and flour.
2. Add ¾ cup (175ml/6fl oz) water and mix again until you have a thick consistency.
3. Heat up a frying pan with a good glug of oil over a high heat and add the mixture in tablespoon-sized amounts. Shallow fry on both sides until golden and crispy.
4. Transfer the cooked bhajis to a plate lined with kitchen towel to absorb any excess oil, and sprinkle a little salt over the top.
5. Finally, add the yoghurt to a bowl and dip the bhajis!

Desserts

Bakewell Tart Fudge

Makes 25–30

Make it, tell no one and hide it in a pot labelled 'Leftover chicken stock' or similar. You'll thank me later!

- 200g (7oz) white chocolate
- 125g (4½oz) almond butter
- 1 handful of glacé cherries, finely diced
- 1 tsp almond extract

1. Add the chocolate to a large microwave-proof bowl and microwave for 2 minutes, stopping every 30 seconds to stir.
2. Once melted, add the almond butter, cherries and almond extract and mix thoroughly.
3. Pour the mixture into a small dish lined with baking paper, and spread out evenly.
4. Place the fudge in the fridge for at least 4 hours, then remove from the dish and peel off the paper. Slice into even squares and that's it!

Salted Caramel Ice Cream

Makes 1 tub

- 1 x 400g (14oz) tin of caramel
- 300ml (10fl oz) double cream
- ½ tsp sea salt flakes

This is lethally good. Lethal, I tell you!

1. Add the double cream to a large bowl. Using an electric whisk, whisk until the cream forms stiff peaks.

2. Fold in the caramel and salt using a spatula so that they are mixed but still have some ripples.

3. Pour the mixture into a freezer-proof container and freeze for a minimum of 8 hours.

Lemon Posset

Makes 4

It's a classic for a reason, and so simple to make! Serve in fancy glasses and everyone will be asking for the recipe.

- 300ml (10fl oz) double cream
- 150g (5oz) caster sugar
- 1 lemon

1. Add the cream and sugar to a saucepan on a low heat and very slowly bring the mixture to a gentle simmer. Stir regularly, until all the sugar has dissolved. As soon as the mixture starts to bubble slightly, turn the heat off. As soon as the mixture starts to bubble slightly, turn the heat off.

2. Add the lemon zest, then the lemon juice and mix thoroughly.

3. Pour the mixture into 4 pots or glasses and leave to set in the fridge for at least 2 hours.

Fruit & Nut Energy Bars

One Bowl

Makes 12

I like to run a small experiment with these. I usually make a batch on a Sunday night and see how long they last. They *should* last until Friday, but they never do! Given how expensive (and sugary) shop-bought cereal bars are, not to mention all the extra packaging, these are something you'll be making on repeat for lunchboxes or snacks. It's hard to go back to dry, dusty ready-made cereal bars once you start making your own.

- 200g (7oz) oats
- 200g (7oz) pitted Medjool dates
- 200g (7oz) smooth peanut butter
- 3 tbsp maple syrup
- 100g (3½oz) dried cranberries

1. Add the oats, dates, peanut butter and maple syrup to a food processor and blitz until combined.
2. Add the cranberries and blitz for 2 or 3 pulses, until the cranberries are combined but not broken down in the mixture.
3. Transfer the mixture to a tray (about 20cm x 30cm) lined with baking paper, and press down evenly.
4. Set aside for 1 hour to allow the mixture to harden up slightly, then remove from the dish, peel off the paper and slice into bars.

No-Bake Chocolate Tart

Serves 8–12

The texture of this tart is like nothing else! Decadent creamy chocolate filling with a fudgy, nutty base – what more could you want from a dessert?

- 200g (7oz) salted peanuts
- 250g (9oz) pitted dates
- 200g (7oz) dark chocolate
- 1 x 400g (14oz) tin of full-fat coconut milk

1. Add the peanuts and dates to a food processor and blitz together until combined.
2. Place the mixture in a tart tin and use the bottom of a glass to push the mixture into the edge and up the side.
3. Add the chocolate to a microwave-proof bowl and melt for 2 to 3 minutes, stopping every 30 seconds to stir. Once melted, add the coconut milk and whisk until combined.
4. Pour the chocolate mixture over the base, and then place the tart in the fridge to set for at least 4 hours.
5. Slice and serve!

No-Bake Peanut Butter Bars

One Bowl

Makes 10–12

A chewy, oaty base with a satisfying thick chocolate crunch across the top. These are a real treat!

- 2 cups (180g/7oz) oat flour
- 1 cup (300g/11oz) peanut butter
- 3 tbsp maple syrup
- 200g (7oz) dark chocolate

1 Combine the oat flour, peanut butter and maple syrup in a large bowl and mix thoroughly.

2 Transfer the mixture to a dish or tray lined with baking paper, and press it down evenly.

3 Add the chocolate to a microwave-proof bowl and microwave for 2 minutes, stopping every 30 seconds to stir. Once melted, pour the mixture over the oats, and then place the dish in the fridge to set for at least 2 hours.

4 Once set, remove from the dish, peel off the paper and slice into bars!

To make the oat flour, add 2 cups (180g/6½oz) regular porridge oats to a food processor and blitz until it looks like flour.

Lemon Curd Cake

Traybake

Serves 8–10

I'm an absolute fiend when it comes to lemon curd. I have to hide the jar from myself whenever I buy any. Which doesn't work because I know where I've hidden it! This soft, buttery lemon sponge is the perfect way to technically 'share' a jar of lemon curd (although there's usually a spoonful or two missing from it in the first place, if you're anything like me...)

- 250g (9oz) self-raising flour
- 60ml (2½fl oz) milk
- 2 eggs
- 100g (3½oz) butter, melted
- 300g (11oz) lemon curd

FOR GREASING
- butter

1 Preheat the oven to 180°C (160°C fan).

2 In a large bowl, combine the flour, milk, eggs, butter and 200g of the lemon curd. Whisk until smooth, then pour the mixture into a well-greased square cake tin (20cm x 20cm) lined with baking paper.

3 Bake for 30 minutes or until a skewer comes out clean, then set aside and leave to cool completely.

4 Using a fork or cocktail stick, poke lots of little holes across the top of the cake. Spread over the remaining lemon curd with a spoon, allowing it to seep into the holes. Slice and enjoy!

Conversion Charts

Liquid measures	
Metric	**Imperial**
1.25ml	¼ tsp
2.5ml	½ tsp
5ml	1 tsp
15ml	1 tbsp
30ml	1fl oz (2 tbsp)
50ml	2fl oz
75ml	3fl oz
100ml	3½fl oz
125ml	4fl oz
150mll	5fl oz (¼ pint)
175ml	6fl oz
200ml	7fl oz
250ml	8fl oz
275ml	9fl oz
300ml	10fl oz
350ml	12fl oz
375ml	13fl oz
400ml	14fl oz
450ml	15fl oz (¾ pint)
475ml	16fl oz
500ml	18fl oz
600ml	20fl oz (1 pint)
700ml	25fl oz (1¼ pints)
850ml	30fl oz (1½ pints)
1 litre	35fl oz (1¾ pints)
1.2 litres	40fl oz (2 pints)
1.3 litres	2¼ pints
1.4 litres	2½ pints
1.75 litres	3 pints
2 litres	3½ pints
3 litres	5 pints

Spoons	
1 tsp	5ml
2 tsp	10ml

Dry weights

Metric	Imperial
10g	¼oz
15g	½oz
20g	¾oz
25g	1oz
40g	1½oz
50g	2oz
60g	2¼oz
70g	2¾oz
75g	3oz
100g	3½oz
115g	4oz
125g	4½oz
140g	4¾oz
150g	5oz
160g	5½oz
175g	6oz
200g	7oz
225g	8oz (½lb)
250g	9oz
275g	9½oz
300g	11oz
350g	12oz
375g	13oz
400g	14oz
425g	15oz
450g	16oz (1lb)
500g	1lb 2oz
550g	1¼lb
600g	1lb 5oz
675g	1½lb
725g	1lb 10oz
800g	1¾lb
850g	1lb 14oz
900g	2lb
1kg	2¼lb
1.1kg	2½lb
1.25kg	2¾lb
1.3kg	3lb
1.5kg	3¼lb

Meal Planner Template

Here is a handy meal planner template, ideal for planning out your own menus. Photocopy it and stick it to your fridge for easy reference.

	M	T
Breakfast		
Lunch		
Dinner		
Dessert		

W	Th	F	Sat	Sun

Recipes by Symbol

Here you've got the recipes by symbol. It's a quick reference guide if you are especially keen on a particular cooking method, like air-frying or traybakes.

One Bowl

Frying Pan

Saucepan

Traybake

Roasting Pot

Air Fryer

Slow Cooker

Recipes by Chapter

Slow and Simple

Sides and Snacks

Desserts

Index

D

E

F

G

H

I

J

K

R

S

T

V

W

Y

Acknowledgements

The writing of this book came at a fairly strange time in my life. I'd just found out I was pregnant, and after eight years of losses and complications to deal with, I wasn't exactly calm and level-headed during the process. But actually, it couldn't have come at a better time because I threw all my energies into writing these recipes whilst eating like a king and filling my freezer with meal prep! I'd like to thank my partner, Tom, first and foremost, for not only taste-testing these meals, but more than any book I've written before, he actually helped create it. We'd sit at the kitchen table and brainstorm together; he helped me come up with half of these recipes and managed to keep me sane when I felt anything but. He wanted to add a whole bunch of offal recipes, but thankfully '15 ways to cook tripe' never got further than our kitchen, you'll be glad to hear... Although, if there's a market for offal cookbooks, Tom is bursting with ideas!

I'd like to thank my wonderful team at HQ, who I've worked with on all three of my books now. It gets easier with every book, because we all know each other, and I feel so grateful to have a team that lets me just crack on but who are always there if I need anything. Particular thanks to Rachael Kilduff, Louise McKeever and Danielle Pender, who have overseen everything and make the world of publishing (a strange and often intimidating place) feel like somewhere I belong and my contributions, valued.

Huge thank you to Liz and Max of Haarala-Hamilton, for the wonderful photographs in this book. The photoshoots are one of the best bits of writing a cookbook and I genuinely adore these two! Liz and Max, and the incredible Rosie Reynolds, Kristine Jakobsson and Poppy Mitchell. Despite being heavily pregnant when we shot these photos and generally a bit overwhelmed, watching these incredible people pull together an entire book in a matter of days is just a joy. There's something balletic about the way they all work together and I'm in awe of them! They usually ask me at the end of every recipe if I'm happy with the final photo, and I always hope I'll find something more useful to say other than, 'It's perfect, I love it', but that's been my initial response to everything they've ever showed me.

Special thanks to Juliet Pickering, my incredible agent. Juliet and I have been working together for four years now and there's nothing I feel I couldn't share with her (both professionally and personally). She was one of the first people I told about this pregnancy, not because it was relevant and not that it changed our schedule in any way but because I trust her implicitly and wanted her to know. The woman is a tonic in my life and I couldn't be without her!

I'd like to thank my mum and dad as well. My mum recently discovered air fryers and lots of the air fryer recipes are inspired by her cooking (she's now one of those people who will tell you how brilliant air fryers are and how you simply MUST get one). Her cheesy leeks even have their own double page spread in this book and you really must try that recipe! My dad is also one of the most passionate foodies I know, and I sent him a few recipes to double-test for me, including the Harissa Chicken with Lemon, Apricot & Pearl Barley, which only works so well because he made sure it did! I grew up eating incredible home-cooked food made by parents who both worked full-time, and hadn't appreciated just how lucky that made me until I became a parent myself!

To my wonderful Instagram community who always come on these journeys with me, be it a cookbook, a pregnancy, a bunch of marathons or perhaps just a camping trip. I was never very good at the whole mums' group thing and wondered if I was just a bit odd because everyone else seemed to have found their 'village'. I needn't have worried though, because I found mine online and there's flipping loads of us! Say what you like about social media, and admittedly it can sometimes be quite trying, the vast majority of people I've been lucky enough to come into contact with have been kinder and more supportive than anything I could have imagined. Seeing my books in your kitchens is the best feeling in the world.

And lastly, as is becoming tradition by now, I'd like to thank my son, Harry. The little (enormous) boy who inspired me to set up a food page four years ago. His short-lived spate of fussiness as a toddler got me cooking with five ingredients in the first place, I jotted down all the successes in a scruffy notepad (literally my first book brought to life) and here we are – three fabulous cookbooks later! As you may know, he is chief recipe-taster and the poor thing often gets the most absurd combinations of things to eat. Sticky Chinese Chicken with a side of Cheesy Gnocchi and perhaps a few savoury pancakes for good measure. He never complains! He's turning into quite the little chef himself, and Tom and I could not be prouder.

HQ
An imprint of HarperCollinsPublishers Ltd
1 London Bridge Street
London SE1 9GF

www.harpercollins.co.uk

HarperCollinsPublishers
Macken House
39/40 Mayor Street Upper
Dublin 1
D01 C9W8
Ireland

10 9 8 7 6 5 4 3 2 1

First published in Great Britain by
HQ, an imprint of HarperCollinsPublishers Ltd 2025

A catalogue record for this book is available from the British Library.

ISBN 978-0-00-864712-4

Publishing Director: Danielle Pender
Senior Editor: Rachael Kilduff
Photographer: Haarala Hamilton Photography
Layout Designer: Studio Nic+Lou
Props Stylist: Aya Nishimura
Food Stylist: Rosie Reynolds
Assistant Food Stylists: Kristine Jakobsson and Poppy Mitchell
Senior Production Controller: Halema Begum

Printed and bound in Bosnia and Herzegovina by GPS Group

For more information visit: www.harpercollins.co.uk/green

When using kitchen appliances please always follow the manufacturer's instructions.